HUMAN RESOURCE POLICIES

Human Resource Policies, Economic Growth, and Demographic Change in Developing Countries

DAVID WHEELER

CLARENDON PRESS · OXFORD

1984

Oxford University Press, Walton Street, Oxford OX2 6DP

London Glasgow New York Toronto
Delhi Bombay Calcutta Madras Karachi
Kuala Lumpur Singapore Hong Kong Tokyo
Nairobi Dar es Salaam Cape Town
Melbourne Auckland

and associated companies in
Beirut Berlin Ibadan Mexico City Nicosia

Oxford is a trade mark of Oxford University Press

Published in the United States
by Oxford University Press, New York

British Library Cataloguing in Publication Data
Wheeler, David
Human resource, policies, economic growth, and
demographic change in developing countries.
1. Manpower policy—Developing countries
2. Manpower planning—Developing countries
I. Title
331.11'09172   HD5852
ISBN 0-19-828459-4

Library of Congress Cataloging in Publication Data
Wheeler, David, 1946-
Human resource policies, economic growth, and
demographic change in developing countries.
Bibliography: p.
Includes index.
1. Economic development—Effect of education on—
Mathematical models.   2. Developing countries—Population
—Mathematical models.   I. Title
HD75.7.W475 1984   338.9'00724   83-20848
ISBN 0-19-828459-4

Typeset by Joshua Associates, Oxford
and printed in Great Britain
by Billing & Sons Ltd, Worcester

For my grandfather

Jesse H. Wheeler
1882–1981.

He believed in education.

PREFACE

There are at least three distinct domains in the academic territory claimed by growth economists. At one end of the territory, theorists work on growth models which are simple enough to yield mathematical solutions. At the other end, simulators construct huge process models which occasionally stray into the territory of science fiction. In the middle domain are the econometricians, who suffer from the contradictory urges which bedevil all centrists. On the one hand, they are willing to be constrained by the data. On the other hand, they acknowledge the need for both rigour (the theorists' product) and relevance (the speciality of the simulators). Theirs is clearly a pitiable task. The suspicion persists, however, that it is a necessary one.

All historians of this territory have noted a pattern of fluctuating importance as the relative populations of the three domains shift in a complex interaction of intellectual births, deaths, and migrations. Attempts to explain this dialectical rhythm have noted the roles played by changing data availability, the evolution of theoretical debate, and the force of public pressure for relevant advice from growth economists. It is plausible to suppose that the territories occupied by other economic subdisciplines (and, indeed, other social sciences) are subject to the same forces of fragmentation and dialectical change.

This book is concerned with growth economics, but it touches on other subjects as well. Since its territorial status is a bit ambiguous, I feel obliged to orient the reader with the aid of a brief chronology. In 1979, I was invited to do research for a contribution to the 1980 World Development Report of the World Bank. At first, my work focused on the relationship between human resource policy and the growth of per capita income in poor countries. If the reader will endure my geographic metaphor a bit longer, I might say that I intended to till the econometric soil near the frontier of the theoretical domain.

Certain compelling forces soon began shifting my position, however. It is hard to explain changes in per capita income without talking about population growth, and once my interest had been piqued I discovered that recent progress in data collection had enhanced the attractiveness of the adjacent territory claimed by demographers. An economic-demographic model, however, has to be built near the domain of the simulators because analytical determinacy can no longer be hoped for.

Thus, my work began near one frontier and ultimately flowed past two others. I do not think that I have spread myself too thin in the process, but the specialized reader may disagree. My own feeling is that the present moment holds great promise for socio-economic growth modelling. Until very recently, problems of data scarcity have frustrated attempts to analyse the role of human resources as 'sources of growth' in less developed countries (LDCs). Similar problems have bedevilled economists and demographers who are trying to identify the main determinants of fertility change in poor countries. With the advent of better data, some progress can now be made.

This book reports and interprets my own efforts, which have three distinguishing characteristics. First, I have been able to estimate a fully simultaneous model of human resource development and economic growth in LDCs. Secondly, the new data have allowed me to estimate a fertility change model which employs only changes in causal variables and which treats change in family planning activity as an endogenous variable. The results are quite strong, and I offer them as one contribution to the continuing discussion of fertility change. Finally, I have cast all of my economic and demographic results into a fully dynamic, data-based simulation model which can project alternative futures for particular countries.

The book is roughly divisible into three parts. In the first part, I present a detailed econometric analysis of the role of human resource development in LDC growth during the past two decades. The second part is devoted to an econometric investigation of declines in fertility and mortality during the same period, with particular attention paid to the contribution of human resource development. In the final part, the simulation model is developed and discussed. The last two chapters use the model to analyse the effects of alternative human resource policies on changes in output and population in countries drawn from different world regions. The demographic projections are compared with recent projections by international agencies, and the book concludes with some thoughts about the potential use of structural modelling in projection exercises.

To the devoted specialist, I know that a book like this one may seem like the Big Muddy—a mile wide and a few feet deep. My own conscience is relatively clear, since I view several parts of the book as considerable research efforts in their own right. In my defence, I might assert that dialogue between academic domains and territories is beneficial for all concerned, and that there is nothing like an attempted sythesis for raising the level (or at least the temperature) of the conversation.

ACKNOWLEDGEMENTS

This book has been several years in the making. Many of my ideas took shape during conversations with colleagues at Boston University, the World Bank, and the Massachusetts Institute of Technology. I cannot hope to recall all of the contributions which others made to my own thinking, but I would certainly like to give credit where I know it is due.

I would like to express my particular appreciation to Paul Isenman, Adrian Wood, Norman Hicks, and Nancy Birdsall of the World Bank, who have read substantial portions of this manuscript and rendered much valuable advice. Thanks are also due to Hollis Chenery, Bevan Waide, and Marcelo Selowsky of the World Bank for their encouragement and helpful comments.

My colleagues and students at Boston University have made many valuable contributions which I would like to acknolwedge. Particular thanks are due to John Harris for many hours of useful discussion. I have also benefited from the insights of Oldrich Kyn, David Morawetz, and Gustav Papanek.

The computer work for this study was largely done at the Information Processing Center of MIT, with funds provided by the World Bank in support of my contribution to the World Development Report in 1980. Substantial word processing time was also provided by the Computer Center of Boston University, and I am grateful to the staffs of both Centers for many kindnesses. Finally, I should acknowledge my debt to the anonymous developers of the SCRIPT word processing software, without which the production of this book would have been vastly more difficult.

CONTENTS

FIGURES

CHAPTER 1

INTRODUCTION

(i) A brief genealogy

In the profession of economics, there has been a persistent tendency to identify population growth as a major hindrance to the process of economic development. Malthus's original vision was a rather bleak one:

> The law of . . . nature . . . implies a strong and constantly operating check on population from the difficulty of subsistence. This difficulty . . . must necessarily be severely felt by a large portion of mankind . . . And the race of man cannot, by any efforts of reason, escape from it . . . misery is an absolutely necessary consequence of it. (Malthus, 1798/1959, p. 5.)

Such a despairing view did not persist among students of Western economies, of course. As the role of the state in those economies began expanding during the early twentieth century, a more limited strain of pessimism emerged. Malthus's acceptance of immiseration was replaced by discussion of the investment opportunity cost associated with the social expenditures needed to support a rapidly growing population. In a recent review article, Perlman (1975) has traced this strain of twentieth-century thought through the work of Fetter (1912), Keynes (1923), Hansen (1939), and Phelps (1972).[1]

When economic theorists began giving more attention to LDCs in the 1950s, however, a sort of neo-Malthusian view asserted itself[2]. During the next two decades, this view was explored in three papers which are the most direct ancestors of my own work. Nelson (1956) made the first attempt to design a mathematical growth model with endogenous population. His results focused on the 'low-level equilibrium trap' which would result if the socio-economic environment produced population growth greater than output growth near the point of subsistence. Although many of Nelson's assumptions were questionable (e.g. linear homogeneity in production; exogeneity of the birthrate), his results did provide an analytical formalization of an important proposition: with low savings rates at low income, the possibility for rapid reduction in the death-rate implies an imbalance between changes in capital and population which can drag an economy inexorably back toward subsistence at a higher level of population. Within Nelson's cloud, however, is a distinctly non-Malthusian silver lining. If a higher income level can be attained by some means, the resulting increase in the savings rate may be more rapid than the associated decrease in the death-rate. Under such happy circumstances the jaws of the low-level equilibrium trap can be sprung open. In Nelson's model, the power of the trap can be reduced by appropriate shifts in exogeneous variables such as the fertility rate, government investment policy, factor productivity, capital inflow, and emigration.

Enke (1963) identified Nelson's result as one case produced by a more general model of population growth and development whose behaviour would ultimately depend upon whether income per capita (presumed to bear a positive relation to the savings rate and a negative relation to the death-rate) was higher at a zero savings rate or a zero population growth rate. He added one crucial assumption to Nelson's set—that general diminishing returns to fixed natural resources must characterize the economy—and showed that the most likely outcome was a 'high-level equilibrium trap' in which population growth balances sustainable investment along a 'zero-improvement curve' dictated by the quality of fixed resources. In the Enke model, shifts in exogeneous factors such as technology, labour efficiency, fertility, and frugality all serve to raise the zero-improvement curve.

The first complete econometric analysis of the Nelson–Enke-type models was not attempted until 1977, for some reason. Hazledine and Moreland (1977) developed a relatively lean model whose equations specified income per capita and a set of other exogeneous variables as determinants of investment, the birth-rate, and the infant mortality rate. The model was fitted by ordinary least-squares to cross-section 1968 data for four major regions (Africa, Latin America, Asia, and the Developed Countries) and the world as a whole. Simulation exercises using 'typical' initial conditions for the four regions were employed to test for the existence of the equilibrium trap. The results seemed to agree with Enke's work:

the . . . hypothesis that there might persist in less developed regions ceiling levels of income per head that will not be exceeded unless some policy action is taken, is given empirical support by our study. (p. 260.)

Taken as a whole, the work of Nelson, Enke, and Hazledine–Moreland is not really as cheerless as the notion of a 'trap' would suggest. All three of these papers assign a useful role to public policy. In the Hazledine–Moreland study, policy interventions are simulated by lowering 'harmful' change rates (e.g. birth-rates) or raising 'helpful' ones (e.g. savings rates) in the first simulation period. For large interventions, the effects look quite hopeful.

While it has certainly defined one of the essential growth problems, existing work on equilibrium traps can be extended in several useful ways. One of the most glaring omissions to date has been the exclusion of all human resource considerations from the analysis. Nelson mentions a possible productivity impact for health improvements in passing; nowhere in the three papers is education mentioned. Presumably, changes in health and education could be lumped together as 'exogenous' forces, but there are some good reasons to suppose that these variables are determined simultaneously with output. Human resource variables apparently have a role to play in the determination of fertility and morality rates, as well.

A second problem common to all three studies is noted by Enke himself:

This analysis, as do those of most economists, ignores some of the complications of population dynamics entailing changes in age distribution. A model that only considers crude birth and death rates provides an approximation at best. A more complicated model should stipulate death and fertility rates for each age bracket and undertake a period by period analysis of population growth and labour availability. (p. 57.)

Several important extensions of the existing work are suggested by this admission.

A third problem is peculiar to the econometric work of Hazledine and Moreland. In their article, each regional model is estimated using a cross-sectional data set, and the results are employed in a set of time series simulations. The pitfalls associated with causal imputation from cross-section regression analyses will be examined in the following chapter. For the present, it suffices to say that the use of time series in this kind of modelling can add a crucial dimension. In addition, it might be noted that regional disaggregation is not necessarily the best approach to estimation when the results are to be used for long-run simulation. The problem can be seen in the following question: are average structural parameters for existing sub-Saharan African economies a better guide to the future than parameters fitted to data which include countries somewhat wealthier than any existing African counterparts? There is no final answer to such a question, but econometric estimation using an inter-regional sample of LDCs may not be such a bad idea.

As always, then, the existing work leaves many gaps to be filled. The model which forms the core of this book attempts to fill several of them. Before moving to specific matters, I should summarize the basic structure of this model and my results.

(ii) The model

The model developed in this book contains both recursive and simultaneous elements. Within growth periods, income, population, and human resource variables change in response to prevailing rates of birth, death, capital accumulation, and labour force growth. These rates are in turn influenced by the full set of induced changes. Because the four crucial stock-adjustment rates are regarded as fixed in the short run, it is convenient to refer to them collectively as 'accumulation parameters'. By the same logic, the human resource measures will join income and population as 'response variables' when a composite reference is required.

In the determination of output growth, the role of human resource variables has been considered in the context of both accumulation and response. In the direct determination of output, the argument that human resource variables have an important role is so plausible as to be beyond argument, at least in a general sense. The Western empirical literature on growth has discerned an important role for education in the growth process, whether its contribution is taken to be labour-augmenting, capital-augmenting, or factor-neutral.[3] Few would doubt that the process of education can have a positive impact on workers' earnings, although there is disagreement about the degree to which the pure role of 'learning' can be divorced from the behavioural effects of 'schooling' and the impact of credentialism.[4]

The case could also be made that health and nutrition are potentially important contributors to productivity in LDCs. Both these factors are undoubtedly characterized by thresholds beyond which their effects on output are negligible. In countries whose populations must endure widespread epidemic illness and nutritional deficiency, however, it is plausible to suppose that productivity is below its potential level with existing stocks of capital and effective labour. The evidence, although relatively scanty, certainly does not suggest a rejection of the hypothesis that these factors can make a difference.[5]

If it is possible to entertain the hypothesis that education, health, and nutrition have an impact on productivity in poor countries, it is of course certain that the opposite is true. Wealthier societies enjoy substantially higher levels of all three variables. In part, this is because higher levels of public investment in health and education are possible in societies which can mobilize more revenue. In addition, increased disposable income allows families to purchase more welfare-enhancing goods and services.

Obviously, it is impossible to evaluate hypotheses concerning the impact of human resource improvements on growth without taking simultaneity explicitly into account. We can therefore characterize a plausible model of the 'response' system as a multi-equation model in which levels of output, education, nutrition, and health are simultaneously determined. In such a system of equations, the stocks of capital and labour would be joined by existing institutional capacity for education and health promotion and other policy variables as exogeneous elements in any particular (short) growth period.

While a 'response' role for human resource variables may be important, they may also have a significant effect on investment behaviour. In this study, both literacy and life expectancy have been hypothesized to join per capita income as determinants of the investment rate. The role of life expectancy is taken to be potentially significant because of life-cycle effects on consumption and savings behaviour. In the case of literacy, a potentially important role can be traced to studies which attribute significant shifts in economic behaviour to the effect of education on attitude formation and economic calculation.[6] For LDCs, it also seems plausible to expect a positive relationship between per capita income and the rate of capital formation, *ceteris paribus*. This hypothesized relationship would follow from the observable decline in marginal propensity to consume as societies shift away from the subsistence margin toward a condition in which some discretionary income is available.

In the preceding brief discussion, attention has been focused on hypothesized relations which tie human resource variables to the process of accumulation and response in output determination. Another plausible set of hypotheses links these variables to demographic changes. The death-rate in any society is linked to the existing institutional and technical capacity for preventive and curative medicine, as well as the prevailing levels of education and income. I have specified a death-rate change equation which attempts to capture these effects. The birth-rate is determined by the proportion in the population of women of reproductive age and their fertility. Since the number of women is exogeneous during any growth period, it is really differences in total fertility rates which must be explained. Unfortunately, there is no generally accepted model to fall back on.[7] For reasons which will be explained in Chapter 4, my model of fertility change includes relatively few variables.

A rough consensus prevails among demographers and population economists that income has a negative effect on fertility in the long run. As income expands, rising opportunity costs seem to outweigh the increasing desire for children, so that women bear fewer babies.[8] Female age at marriage should also have an impact on fertility, since there is a close link between marriage and child-bearing in most cultures.

Part of this impact is physiological: increased age at marriage reduces the number of child-bearing years, and particularly those in which fecundity is highest. Part of the impact may also have to do with attitudinal change in women who have more experience of life before marriage. It is plausible to suppose that age at marriage is, in turn, a function of education, income, and life expectancy. Education itself may have a direct impact on fertility decisions.[9] Educated women perceive higher opportunity costs; they may be more willing and able to plan for the future; and they may have greater knowledge of and receptivity to modern contraceptive methods.

The three variables mentioned above are all presumed to have an impact on the desired number of children. In LDCs, of course, the children of the poor are at considerable risk. At a fixed desired level of family size, lower infant mortality lowers the risk and should (at least in the long run) lower fertility. Infant morality is therefore assigned a causal role in the fertility equation.[10]

To the 'demand' variables affecting fertility there should be appended a 'supply' variable: the cost and availability of family planning services. A cross country index of intensity in family planning activities, recently employed by Mauldin and Berelson (1978), has been included in the equation.[11] For a variety of reasons, it seems plausible to suppose that family planning activity itself is determined simultaneously with fertility decline. The full model therefore includes a family planning equation which relates change in this activity to change in the fertility rate and a proxy for institutional capacity (the secondary school enrolment ratio).

(iii) The data

Until fairly recently, the data available for cross country examination of relations between human resources and growth have simply been insufficient for econometric work. An additional problem has been posed by the degree to which macro-level cross-section results are believable. Cross country comparisons of value-based data such as gross domestic product (GDP) statistics are suspect in many ways, and problems of data scarcity have prevented the application of some compensatory techniques in the past. In cross-section work, there is also the problem of masked correlations, so that even results which seem to corroborate maintained hypotheses about causal relations can frequently be explained with reference to other, unobserved variables. Finally, the evident presence of simultaneity in the determination of socio-economic outcomes has always presented a major stumbling-block to the pursuit of consistent and believable research in this domain.

In the project whose results are being reported here, all of these problems were evident from the beginning. A major part of the research effort has therefore been devoted to overcoming them, in so far as this has been perceived to be possible. In all cases, an attempt has been made to move toward believability in results by estimating regression equations with cross country changes rather than levels. This use of change relations has yielded one additional advantage: among plausible models of output determination, several have an intertemporal specification in percentage change form. In a cross-section of time series, the calculation of percentage changes within countries avoids the index number problems which plague many cross country studies.

Even when a cross-section of time series is employed, of course, it is not possible to give an unambiguous interpretation to econometric results in most cases. Masked correlations may still be present, and it would be rare to find a case in which at least one alternative explanation for observed results could not be imagined. In addition, the use of relatively scanty data and the necessity for some experimentation in the evaluation of alternative functional forms and the testing of variables which seem plausible a priori increase the risk that any single set of regression results is simply a sampling accident.

For this reason, considerable time and effort have been expended in the attempt to cross-check the data in a variety of ways. Identical models of behaviour for the 1960s and the 1970s have been estimated separately for the output response equations, since this part of the model is most subject to the difficulties associated with the simultaneity problem and the possible effect of intervening variables. This same set of equations has been re-estimated with whole world regions excluded, to test for the possibility that apparently 'general' phenomena are in fact traceable to the characteristics of a particular region. Finally, a substantial set of plausible intervening variable effects has been hypothesized, and the fundamental equations have been rerun to see whether the originally specified relations seemed to remain once other factors were accounted for.

(iv) Principal findings

With all this as prelude, it is undoubtedly fitting to conclude this introduction with a summary of the principal findings of the research. In the response component of the output equations, simultaneous equation estimating techniques have been employed throughout. The results have suggested the confirmation of some prior hypotheses and the rejection of others. As anticipated, changes in per capita income across countries seem to have a significant, positive impact on changes in literacy and life expectancy. In addition, a positive impact is suggested for calorie consumption, which can be interpreted as the best single available measure of general nutritional status. None of the direct links from per capita income to social indicator variables is particularly surprising, although the results have the advantage of being based on changes rather than levels.

Of more potential interest in the simultaneous estimates is the evaluation of hypotheses concerning the impact of the social indicator variables on output growth. In each case, as previously mentioned, there is a plausible argument for some contribution to productivity.

After an exhaustive series of tests over different time periods, with various regional exclusions, and with the use of many plausible intervening variables to test for continued significance, a relatively clear set of conclusions has emerged. The impact of literacy change on output change is apparent in all the tests which have been run. When life expectancy change is used as a proxy for health improvement, however, no consistent results are obtained. In simultaneous estimates for the 1960s, changes in life expectancy appear to contribute significantly to changes in output. In the 1970s, however, the effect is reversed: the variable loses significance and in fact exhibits a negative relationship with output change in the simultaneous estimates. It seems appropriate to conclude that the results for the 1960s may have been a sampling accident, and that life expectancy as a proxy for health cannot be identified as a significant contributor to productivity growth.[12]

Although education and health are really the focus of attention here, it is of interest to examine the hypothesized impact of nutrition on productivity. The results of all the econometric exercises certainly lend support to this hypothesis, if the available index of nutrition is acceptable as a proxy. After simultaneity has been explicitly accounted for, changes in calorie consumption appear to have a significant impact on output changes across countries. It must be noted, however, that the calorie variable may be serving as a proxy for relative changes in agricultural productivity. Some development economists have maintained that agricultural growth has a differential impact on output growth, and the observed result may be in part an indirect confirmation of this hypothesis. At the present time, there does not seem to be any good way of separating the two effects.

As previously noted, plausible hypotheses link human resource variables with accumulation parameters as well as response variables in the growth system. In the case of output growth, an association can be hypothesized between levels of education and life expectancy and the investment rate in LDCs. Such a link, if established, would suggest an indirect role for the available health measure in the generation of productivity change, as well as an additional role for education.

Again, econometric work on the relationship between the investment rate and various causal variables has yielded mixed conclusions. Time series work in this particular context has not been plentiful in the past, and in this project it was hypothesized that the effects which were being tested might show up only over relatively long periods if at all, given the substantial measurement problems which exist. In the case of the investment rate, regression equations were fitted to data on changes in the investment rate across LDCs during the period 1960–77. The results suggest relatively strong roles for per capita income and literacy in the determination of this rate. The result for life expectancy is extremely weak when it is used along with literacy in the investment rate equation, although the coefficient of the life expectancy term satisfies the usual statistical criteria when literacy is excluded. At best, any hypothesized role for life expectancy in the determination of relative investment rates is cast into doubt by these results.

In the demographic component of the modelling exercise, the results are similarly mixed. As previously mentioned, part of the variation in birth-rates across countries can be attributed to differing proportions of young women in their populations. There is obviously a component of the death-rate which is sensitive to age structure differentials as well. Once this deterministic component is accounted for, both rates can plausibly be related to several human resource and policy variables. Technical and institutional capacity should have an effect on the death-rate, as should changes in the level of health-promoting consumption at higher income levels. Other variables such as nutrition and education might be supposed to have some effect, as well. In the case of fertility rates, such variables as income, infant mortality rates, and appropriate family planning efforts could certainly be suggested as causal. A potential complication is raised by the possibility that family planning activity begins more readily in countries which have already exhibited some decline in fertility rates, because of encouragement effects.

In econometric work on birth- and death-rate determination, regression equations were fitted to seventeen-year changes to allow for periods of time sufficient to overcome the effects of measurement error. In both cases, the data allowed for explicit testing of the hypothesis that the causal variables had differential effects in different age cohorts. In the case of fertility rates, estimation was further complicated by the necessity of allowing for explicitly simultaneous determination of fertility rates and family planning activity.

Among the variables which might plausibly have been related to changes in death-rates and fertility rates, those mentioned above all appear to play a significant role. In the case of death-rate changes, only the availability of medical personnel as indexed by doctors per capita appears to account for effects beyond those attributable to a strong autonomous technical change component.

In the simultaneous equation estimates, an important role in fertility rate determination is suggested for per capita income, the death-rate (which is a proxy for unavailable infant mortality rate data), and the level of family planning activity. The last, in turn, seems well explained by contemporaneous declines in the fertility rate and the institutional capacity of the society in question (for which the secondary school enrolment ratio is used as a proxy). The results certainly do not lead to a rejection of the hypothesis that fertility decline contributes significantly to the initiation of family planning activity across countries, for whatever reason. In addition, the fertility results suggest that the marginal effects of causal variables across age cohorts cannot be differentiated from one another at a high level of statistical confidence, although cohort-specific constant terms naturally differ.

The impact of singulate age at marriage (SAM), i.e. the age at marriage of females who have not been married previously, on fertility rates could not be measured in the time-change equation because data were insufficient. However, this variable was tested in a set of separate equations fitted to the combined pool of data for the years 1960 and 1977 in order to maximize degrees of freedom. The results suggest that age at marriage is well accounted for by literacy and life expectancy. When all three variables are included in a cross-section regression, the residual component of age at marriage seems to account for no additional variance in the fertility rate.

In the aftermath of a relatively complex set of econometric estimation exercises, it is always of interest to examine the dynamic behaviour implied by the full set of equations. As previously mentioned, the equation system whose parameters have been estimated is too complex for the calculation of fixed multipliers. Simulation is thus the relevant tool for analysis and prediction. In Chapter 8, some experiments with educational policy are used to test for the existence of a 'low-level equilibrium trap' when human resource variables are included as sources of growth in prototypical African and South Asian societies. The results seem consistent with the presumed existence of such a trap only when educational progress is entirely suppressed. Chapter 9 investigates the cost effectiveness of human resource investments. Simulated time paths for the physical quality of life (PQLI) variables (income, literacy, nutrition, and life expectancy) are compared for roughly cost-equivalent increases in schooling, family planning, and physical investment. The comparisons suggest that judgements about relative cost effectiveness vary with initial conditions, the weights attached to different PQLI outcomes, and the discount rate.

In the final chapters, data for several LDCs are introduced as initial conditions for the simulation model and different levels of human resource investment are used to project future demographic patterns. These are compared with recent demographic projections by the United Nations and the World Bank, and substantial differences are revealed. The book closes with a discussion of the reasons for these differences and an appeal for greater use of structural modelling by the international projection agencies.

PART I

HUMAN RESOURCES AND OUTPUT GROWTH

CHAPTER 2

SOCIO-ECONOMIC GROWTH:
A SIMULTANEOUS MODEL

(i) Some technical problems

It would be incorrect to assert that no empirical work has focused on the effects of basic human resource development on productivity across countries in the 1970s. Some analysts have done cross-section studies of the intercorrelation among measures of economic performance, public policy decisions, and basic social indicators. Work in this area has been plagued by several recurring problems, however. In the first place, most of the published studies are static exercises. That is, they attempt to draw inferences about causality within countries from data which have only been taken across countries. Since many socio-economic indices are roughly correlated, it is relatively easy to obtain good cross-section results which tempt the researcher to draw broad policy conclusions.

As any practising econometrician who has worked in this area can affirm, unfortunately, cross country correlation and within-country causality are definitely two different things. Characteristically, regression exercises which suggest high degrees of intercorrelation in cross-section lose most of their 'explanatory power' when within-country changes are considered.[13] And yet, this type of modelling exercise must in the final analysis be concerned with changes. Most professional economists are unlikely to be persuaded by cross-section regressions estimated on levels alone.

The second weakness of the existing work is the prevailing assumption of one-way causation. Variables such as basic education are presumed to have an effect on output, but not conversely. At the very least, however, a well-specified growth model should be explicitly simultaneous in changes in output, nutrition, and education. Such a model would include indices for these three endogenous variables, as well as a relatively large set of predetermined variables. If sufficient data were available, unbiased, efficient estimates for the parameters of the simultaneous equations could be obtained with the aid of systems estimation techniques such as three-stage least-squares.[14] Unfortunately, the spottiness of the data presents a third problem.

The available World Bank data for 88 countries measure levels of various socio-economic indices at three points in time: 1960, 1970, and 'the mid-1970s' (1974 through 1977 in individual cases). The most recent data are fairly plentiful, but there are still many gaps in the full 88-country matrix for the mid-1970s. As the data move back in time, they get spottier. The result is that measurable changes in key indices are rarer than corresponding levels. In a simultaneous model, many of the crucial changes must be taken from the same set of countries. Only the intersection of available measures counts. The size of this intersection diminishes steadily as the number of simultaneously-measured changes mounts, and the result can be disastrous for system-modelling techniques such as three-stage least-squares.

Thus, reality once again presents the econometrician with a situation which has not been anticipated in the textbooks. The need for a simultaneous model and the need to measure model variables in changes are in clear conflict with one another here. For equations which are not explicitly part of the simultaneous system, simple linear equation techniques will suffice, and each equation can be fitted using the data which are needed for it alone. To the extent that simultaneity is abandoned, degrees of freedom in estimation will be maximized for individual equations in the model. At the same time, the artificial decoupling of truly simultaneous relations will result in inconsistent parameter estimates in the equations in question. Since the spottiness of the data cannot be remedied, this problem cannot be avoided. Some compromise has therefore been unavoidable in model specification.

(ii) Output modelling in a simultaneous context

In this chapter, attention is focused on a simultaneous four-equation model whose jointly-determined variables are output, nutrition, education and health. The general form of the model (for a particular country in period t) is given by:

(1a) $Q\{t\} = Q[K\{t\}, L'(L\{t\}, N\{t\}, E\{t\}, H\{t\}), A\{t\}]$

(1b) $N\{t\} = N[(Q/P\{t\}, (Q/P)\{t-1\}, \ldots]$

(1c) $E\{t\} = E[(Q/P\{t\}, S\{t-k\}, S\{t-k-1\}, \ldots]$

(1d) $H\{t\} = H[(Q/P)\{t\}, N\{t\}, N\{t-1\}, \ldots, E\{t\},$
$$E\{t-1\}, \ldots, G\{t\}, G\{t-1\}, \ldots]$$

where
Q = Output
P = Population
K, L' = Use levels of capital and augmented labour services
L = Labour services

N = Nutrition per worker
E = Basic education per worker
A = An index of technical progress
S = A measure of past schooling for the current labour force[15]
G = A set of measures of present and past health services provided
H = A measure of health status per worker

The first equation is a generalized form of the production function which incorporates the labour-augmenting effects of health, nutrition, and education. The three social indicator equations reflect the income-elasticity of consumption patterns which promote nutrition, education, and health. They are themselves quasi-reduced-form equations, since per capita income enters as the primary determinant of demand and the associated supply conditions are taken to be either perfectly elastic (1b) or exogenously determined (1(c), 1(d)).

In 1(b), where the link is obviously through the income-elastic demand for food, the potential availability of imports is taken to imply a flat nutrient supply curve. Equation 1(c) presumes that the demand for adult education is income-responsive, while past provision of educational services to children contributes to the current educational level of the labour force. In 1(d), present and past nutrition levels are assumed to have an impact on health. Present and past education also enter, through their effect on dietary and sanitary practices. In addition, the demand for other goods and services which are health-promoting (e.g., safe water, sanitation systems, fly screens) is taken to be income elastic, so that a direct impact of per capita income on health should be observable. On the supply side, the level of public provision of health personnel and facilities is included.

(iii) Specification issues

Since the proposed growth model is explicitly simultaneous, the four equations must be specified compatibly. Existing work provides little guidance for the imposition of particular functional forms on the social indicator equations. The properties of alternative production functions, on the other hand, are quite familiar. Attention has therefore been focused on the production equation, with the social indicator equations specified in the form which is appropriate for system estimation.

In modelling the production process, it is necessary to give simultaneous attention to the roles of factor-augmenting inputs and to the roles of effective capital and labour in determining output. In the determination of effective labour, the contributions of nutrition and health are assumed to be characterized by unitary elasticity of substitution. The contribution of education, on the other hand, is specified log-linearly. The partial equation for augmented labour is as follows. (The symbol ★★ denotes exponentiation; percentage changes are denoted by ⟨⟩; subscripts by { }.)

(2) $L'\{t\} = L\{t\} \star (N\{t\}\star\star b1) \star \exp(E\{t\}\star b2) \star (H\{t\}\star\star b2)$

Two alternative specifications of the production function have been considered:

(3a) Augmented Constant Elasticity of Substitution (CES)

$Q\{t\} = A\{t\} \star [a\star(K\{t\}\star\star p) + |(1-a)\star(L'\{t\}\star\star p)] \star\star(1/p)$

where
a, p = CES parameters

(3b) Augmented Cobb–Douglas:

$Q\{t\} = A\{t\} \star (K\{t\}\star\star g1) \star (L'\{t\}\star\star g2)$

Empirical testing has yielded the conclusion that (3a) is not significantly better than (3b) as a representation of production in this case. Thus production is assumed to exhibit the following behaviour throughout:

(4) $Q\{t\} = A\{t\} \star (K\{t\}\star\star g1) \star [L\{t\} \star (N\{t\}\star\star b1) \star \exp(E\{t\}\star b2)$
$\star (H\{t\}\star\star b3)] \star\star g2$

Here $g1$ and $g2$ can be interpreted as the output elasticities of capital and effective labour, while the b's are labour-augmenting parameters for nutrition, education, and health.

Equation (4) would be appropriate for estimation if time series for a single country were being considered. In this case, however, only two primary observations (for 1970 and the mid-1970s) are available for each country in the sample, along with one additional set of past observations (for 1960). The model must therefore be specified to reflect the consequences of single-period changes across countries. The time derivative of (4) is used as the production equation.

(5) $\langle dq \rangle = \langle dA \rangle + g1\star\langle dk \rangle + g2\star\langle d1 \rangle + g2\star b1\star\langle dn \rangle + g2\star b2\star\langle de \rangle$
$+ g2\star b3\star\langle dh \rangle$

where $\langle dx \rangle = [dx\{t\}/dt]/x\{t\}$

This equation is linear in percentage changes, with the exception of the literacy component (which is linear in changes). For compatibility, identical change specifications have been imposed on the social indicator equations.[16] Since the literacy equation has been specified appropriately in absolute changes, however, it requires a little more attention. The functional form employed here follows directly from an explicit specification of the process of 'literacy production'.

The variable which is basically of interest in this context is the number of literate adult members of the labour force. Some of these adults may well educate themselves, and we would expect the demand for self-education (or for commerical forms of adult instruction) to be positively related to per capita income. For the vast majority of adults, however, literacy will have come about as a result of primary schooling.

For two time periods ($\{t\}$ and $\{t-1\}$), then, we can model the increase in the number of literate adults as:

(6) $LAD\{t\} - LAD\{t-1\} = Pr(E) \star S \star [AD\{t\} - AD\{t-1\}]$

where
LAD = Number of literate adults
AD = Number of adults
S = Primary school enrolment ratio during the period when the adult age cohort received primary schooling
$Pr(E)$ = Probability that some experience of schooling results in literacy

We know that the adult literacy rate is equal to the ratio (LAD/AD). Some mathematical manipulation therefore gives us the following relationship:

(7) $E\{t\} - E\{t-1\} \star [1/(1 + \langle da \rangle)] = Pr(E) \star S \star [\langle da \rangle/(1 + \langle da \rangle)]$

where
E = The adult literacy rate
$\langle da \rangle$ = Percentage change in the adult population from $\{t-1\}$ to t

With the addition of change in per capita income and a constant term, the model of literacy change is complete.

(iv) Measurement problems

The data for this study have been drawn from 88 poor countries in Africa, Asia, Southern America, and Southern Europe. In most cases, the variables employed for estimation can only be defended as the best available. The input and output measures in the three human resource response equations are all national averages, so that substantial differences in distribution are masked by the data. This problem is apt to be more severe for the measurement of availability of medical personnel than for the other indices. Aggregative measures of population per doctor say nothing about differences in the length or efficacy of training programmes or the geographical distribution of medical personnel within countries. Thus, this measure is not very satisfactory as an index of generalized access to medical care.

The measures of nutrition and education, on the other hand, may not be too bad. As a measure of nutritional status per capita, calorie availability is a reasonable approximation. It is now generally accepted that calorie sufficiency is much more likely to indicate nutritional adequacy than any other index. At the same time, available microeconomic studies always show a rapid drop in the income elasticity of calorie consumption across income classes within countries, so that it is reasonable to link expansion in calorie consumption with increases in the nutritional status of the poor as per capita income rises.[17] Among measures of the change in basic education, the change in the adult literacy rate is undoubtedly the best available index.

The conventional economic indices in the study are subject to many of the usual strengths and weaknesses. The measured change in gross domestic product seems acceptable, as does the change in total population. The way in which $\langle dk \rangle$ and $\langle d1 \rangle$ are employed in the simple production model is unfortunately much less satisfactory. The use of percentage changes in capital and labour in a production model incorporates the assumption of constant utilization of the available services. This is obviously wrong (and particularly so for labour in poor countries), but nothing can be done about it because reliable information on capacity utilization rates and unemployment rates for these countries simply does not exist.

In addition, the available labour force data seem to be very unreliable. As a result, the growth rate in the labour force employed in this book is indexed by the growth rate in the adult population. Although admittedly crude, this index at least is based on data which have been gathered with relative accuracy. It would be difficult to argue that it does not capture the dominating age cohort effect in labour force growth. At the same time, the use of percentage changes in the model makes the implicit exclusion of the labour force participation rate much less damaging, since it is likely to remain relatively constant over short periods and therefore washes out of a percentage change measure.

An additional complication is introduced by the complete non-availability of reliable and comparable capital stock figures for these countries, so that it is impossible to obtain direct measures of percentage changes for the period 1960-77. Available data on yearly investment and output do allow for estimation under the assumption (admittedly heroic) that the general capital/output ratio for the countries in question did not change significantly during the estimation periods. Some manipulation of the production model yields:

$$[dQ/dt]/Q\{o\} = [dA/dt]/A\{o\} + g11\star[Q\{o\}/K\{o\}]\star[(dK/dt)/Q\{o\}] + g12\star[dL'/dt]/L'\{o\}$$

or

(8) $\quad \langle dq \rangle = \langle dA \rangle + g11\star[(Q/K)\star\langle dk \rangle] + g12\star\langle d1' \rangle$

where

Q = Output
A = An appropriate index of technical progress
K = Capital
L = Labour
$\langle dq \rangle, \langle dk \rangle$ = As previously defined
$\langle dA \rangle$ = Percentage change in technical progress index
$\langle d1' \rangle$ = Percentage change in effective (augmented) labour
$\{o\}$ = Initial period

Since we can observe $[(dK/dt)/Q\{o\}]$, estimation with some unknown degree of bias is possible. It is comforting to note that the mean capital/output ratio must be somewhere in the range 2-5 and the combined output elasticities for capital and effective labour can be somewhat greater than one at most, so the econometric results must conform to certain obvious restrictions.

A final cautionary note concerns the inevitable masking of sectoral and institutional detail in an aggregative growth accounting exercise. Because changes in capital, labour, and human resources may have impacts which differ by sector, aggregative elasticity estimates should properly be interpreted as measures of central tendency. They are not likely to be a major source of error for simulated comparisons of societies which are roughly similar in sectoral composition (such as those considered in Chapter 10). It is entirely possible that major institutional differences across societies also have an effect on the degree to which human resource improvements alter labour productivity. While 'institutional considerations' may be significant, a clearer view of their precise nature will have to emerge before quantification becomes practicable.[18]

CHAPTER 3

ECONOMETRIC RESULTS

(i) The basic model

Having surveyed the theoretical terrain, we can pass to the equation set which has actually been estimated. As noted, the output equation is basically derived from the Cobb-Douglas function. This log-linear specification, when translated to time-change form, is linear in percentage changes in model variables. Thus, a specification of the input-output relationship suggested by our basic hypotheses concerning the contribution of human resources to growth at the macro-level would look like the following:[19]

$$(9) \quad \langle dq \rangle = a0 + a1 \star \langle dk \rangle + a2 \star \langle dl \rangle + a3 \star \langle dh \rangle + a4 \star \langle dn \rangle + a5 \star \langle de \rangle + u$$

where

$\langle dq \rangle$ = Change in output
$\langle dk \rangle$ = Change in capital
$\langle dl \rangle$ = Change in the labour force
$\langle dh \rangle$ = Change in health status
$\langle dn \rangle$ = Change in nutrition status
$\langle de \rangle$ = Change in education
u = A random error term

In the output equations which have actually been estimated for this study, data problems have necessitated some departures from the pure Cobb-Douglas form. As previously noted, capital stock data across countries are simply unavailable and the variable actually employed in the equations is the intra-period change in capital (investment), divided by the initial level of output.

The second major departure from the form implied by the Cobb-Douglas specification is the substitution of the intra-period change in literacy for the intra-period percentage change as the measure of basic educational improvement. This substitution is intended to solve a significant measurement problem. During a period in which many countries have moved from extremely low literacy to somewhat higher levels, modest absolute gains translate to huge percentage changes. The result for econometrics is that a relatively small number of countries which began at very low literacy levels in 1960 can dominate the entire sample numerically. It has therefore been deemed desirable to use absolute differences for literacy change. In theoretical terms, this translates to a model which is very similar to the Cobb–Douglas except that the effect of education enters as a multiplicative exponential rather than a multiplicative power of education itself.

The other equations of the output model have been specified in a way which dovetails with the specification of the output equation. For the available measures of nutrition and health, percentage changes have been employed. In addition, the nutrition change equation incorporates a term which captures some delay in the adjustment of current consumption to per capita income, while the life expectancy change equation incorporates terms to capture the effects of nutrition, education, and the availability of medical personnel.

Because the contribution of literacy to output change has been modelled using absolute changes, the literacy change equation has been specified in compatible form. This equation measures the marginal effect of per capita income growth on the growth of literacy as well as the actual effect of schooling on the age cohort which passes to adulthood in each period. In the regression equation, the coefficient of the appropriately modified schooling variable can be interpreted as the measured probability that a child who attended primary school during the period in question actually became literate in the process. In the life expectancy equation, an index of medical personnel availability is used to capture the effect of public health efforts on life expectancy change.

Both the availability indices mentioned above represent service intensity levels which make contributions to changes in endogenous variables. At first glance this may seem inappropriate, since an adequate causal model must in the final analysis relate changes to changes. This remains true for the current exercise, but service levels are crucial intermediaries. In the literacy equation, for example, the change in adult literacy is mainly due to the result of a 'throughput' process. Children have passed through primary education facilities (whose capacity is represented by the primary enrolment ratio), and some have emerged literate. Thus, an autonomous flow (children) through service institutions whose capacity is defined, results in a changed condition of literacy for the adult population.

This same 'throughput' notion applies to all equations in the response model except the output equation. In the life expectancy equation, the flow in question is health technology. For a poor country, the degree to which a constantly improving technology can be applied depends upon the availability of appropriate channels. One channel is clearly the set of potential services defined by available medical personnel and facilities. Another is associated with the means for effectively conveying public health information. Undoubtedly, primary

HUMAN RESOURCE POLICIES

FIGURE 1
Output Equation Results—Closed Economy Model (*)

1960-1970

Observations

$$\langle dq \rangle = .052 + .142\star\langle dk \rangle + .301\star\langle dl \rangle + .869\star\langle dn \rangle$$
$$\quad (.124)\ (.034) \qquad (.319) \qquad (.440)$$

$$\quad + .016\star[E\{t\} - E\{t-1\}]$$
$$\quad (.005)$$

39

$$\langle dn \rangle = -.057 + [4.215 - .868\star\ln N]\star[\langle dq \rangle - \langle dp \rangle]$$
$$\quad (.022)\ \ (1.031)\ (.222)$$

$$\quad + .038\star\ln[(Q/P)/N]$$
$$\quad (.020)$$

39

$$E\{t\} - E\{t-1\}\star[1/(1+\langle da \rangle)] = -2.423 + .988\star S\star[\langle da \rangle/(1+\langle da \rangle)]$$
$$\qquad\qquad\qquad\qquad\qquad (2.259)\ (.137)$$

$$\qquad\qquad\qquad\qquad\qquad + 8.313\star[\langle dq \rangle - \langle dp \rangle]$$
$$\qquad\qquad\qquad\qquad\qquad (3.697)$$

39

1970-1977

$$\langle dq \rangle = -.109 + .182\star\langle dk \rangle + .592\star\langle dl \rangle + .557\star\langle dn \rangle$$
$$\quad (.079)\ (.036) \qquad (.337) \qquad (.390)$$

$$\quad + .0080\star[E\{T\} - E\{t-1\}]$$
$$\quad (.0037)$$

43

$$\langle dn \rangle = -.033 + [4.450 - .948\ln N]\star[\langle dq \rangle - \langle dp \rangle]$$
$$\quad (.016)\ \ (1.370)\ (.292)$$

$$\quad + .051\star\ln[(Q/P)/N]$$
$$\quad (.014)$$

43

$$E\{t\} - E\{t-1\}\star[1/(1+\langle da \rangle)] = 2.985 + .639\star S\star[\langle da \rangle/(1+\langle da \rangle)]$$
$$\qquad\qquad\qquad\qquad\qquad (2.045)\ (.174)$$

$$\qquad\qquad\qquad\qquad\qquad + 14.485\star[\langle dq \rangle - \langle dp \rangle]$$
$$\qquad\qquad\qquad\qquad\qquad (4.248)$$

43

POOLED DATA

$$\langle dq \rangle = [.012 - .087\star D70] + .146\star\langle dk \rangle + .565\star\langle dl \rangle$$
$$\quad (.088)\ (.048) \qquad\quad (.025) \qquad (.239)$$

$$\quad + 1.011\star\langle dn \rangle + .0096\star[E\{t\} - E\{t-1\}].$$
$$\quad (.417) \qquad (.0037)$$

82

$\langle dn \rangle = [-.040 + .009 \star D70] + [3.259 - .674 \ln N] \star [\langle dq \rangle - \langle dp \rangle]$
 (.017) (.016) (.894) (.191)

 + .042$\star \ln [(Q/P)/N]$. 82
 (.012)

$E\{t\} - E\{t-1\} \star [1/(1 + \langle da \rangle)] = [-.996 + 3.986 \star D70] $ 82
$\phantom{E\{t\} - E\{t-1\} \star [1/(1 + \langle da \rangle)] = [}$ (2.265) (1.810)

$\phantom{E\{t\} - E\{t-1\} \star [1/(1 + \langle da \rangle)] =}$ + .755$\star S \star [\langle da \rangle /(1 + \langle da \rangle)]$
$\phantom{E\{t\} - E\{t-1\} \star [1/(1 + \langle da \rangle)] =}$ (.138)

$\phantom{E\{t\} - E\{t-1\} \star [1/(1 + \langle da \rangle)] =}$ + 12.291$\star [\langle dq \rangle - \langle dp \rangle]$.
$\phantom{E\{t\} - E\{t-1\} \star [1/(1 + \langle da \rangle)] =}$ (4.188)

LIFE EXPECTANCY CHANGE, 1970–1977

$\langle dh \rangle = -.124 + 6.948 \star (1/H) + [.573 - .144 \ln H] \star [\langle dq \rangle - \langle dp \rangle] $ R$\star\star$2
 (.038) (1.570) (.290) (.072) 52 .63

 + .142$\star \langle dh\{t-1\} \rangle$ + .077$\star \langle dn\{t-1\} \rangle$ + .027$\star [E/H]$
 (.082) (.027) (.012)

 − 1.10$E-5 \star [M/H]$ + .010$\star [S/H]$.
 (.70$E-5$) (.006)

VARIABLE DEFINITIONS

$\langle dq \rangle$, $\langle dl \rangle$, $\langle dh \rangle$, $\langle dn \rangle$, $\langle dp \rangle$, $\langle da \rangle$ = Percentage changes in real GDP, labour, life ex-
 pectancy, nutrition, population, and adult
 population, respectively

$\langle dk \rangle$ = [Change in capital] /initial GDP

$E\{t-1\}$, $E\{t\}$ = Literacy rate in initial and final years of estimation period,
 respectively

$\ln N$, $\ln H$ = Logarithms of initial nutrition and life expectancy levels

Q/P = Initial level of per capita income

S = Previous primary school enrolment ratio relevant for the newest adult age
 cohort

$D70$ = Dummy variable with values [0 = 1960–70, 1 = 1970–77]

H = Initial life expectancy level

M = Initial availability of medical personnel

E (In life expectancy equation) = Initial literacy rate

(*) Standard errors in parentheses beneath coefficients.

schooling is important in this process, as are various printed media. Thus, both the primary school enrolment ratio and the adult literacy rate are defensible indices of information-transfer capacity.

A look at the global evidence for the past two decades also suggests that there has been a sizeable and near-universal rise in life expectancy which has been due to widespread mass vaccinations and other internationally subsidized technologies. For any country, then, there should be a substantial component of life expectancy change which is simply 'autonomous'. Since countries may well differ with respect to their ability to implement such universally available health measures, it makes sense to suppose that life expectancy change in the 1970s should exhibit some lagged relationship with the change in the 1960s for a particular country. A lagged adjustment term has therefore been included in the life expectancy equation.

In the interests of completeness, three sets of basic regression results are presented here. As a fairly stringent test of the underlying hypothesis concerning the direct contribution of human resource variables to growth, the same model was run on data for the 1960s, data for the 1970s, and a set which pooled data for both periods. The initial results made it clear that life expectancy as a measure of health has no consistent impact on output growth, although the reverse phenomenon is apparent. Because the exclusion of life expectancy change from the output equation and the consequent decoupling of the life expectancy change equation from the simultaneous system allowed for a significant saving in degrees of freedom in estimation, the basic model presented here (Figure 1) is in three-equation simultaneous form.[20]

The three sets of estimates presented in Figure 1 seem to tell a consistent story.[21] Capital, labour, literacy, and the measure of nutritional adequacy all show up in the output equation in both periods with the expected sign, reasonable magnitudes, and a general pattern of adequacy by an appropriate one-tailed criterion. An exception is posed by the labour coefficient in the period 1960–70. Since it does not seem plausible to suppose that labour has no effect on output in any case, attention should be focused on the magnitude of the estimated coefficient itself.

In interpreting the results for the output equation, it is important to recall that the capital stock change variable is really the total change in capital during the estimation period divided by the initial output level. Interpretation of the resulting coefficient depends upon an independent estimate of the capital/output ratio. Generally, the estimation results seem consistent with a capital/output ratio of about 3 and constant returns to scale. The implied capital and labour shares are not radically different from those found in econometric estimates for the industrial societies.[22]

As mentioned in the introduction, some ambiguity attaches to the 'nutrition' coefficient which accompanies the percentage change in calorie consumption. In part, this result may represent the beneficial impact of rapid agricultural growth, which has been pointed to by numerous development economists as a potential source of differential productivity in LDCs. It might well be over-optimistic to attribute all of the measured impact to nutrition, although it is certainly plausible to suppose that some of the effect is due to this variable.[23]

In summary, the results for simultaneously-estimated response equations are consistent with two of the basic hypotheses which were of interest to this study—that basic nutrition and education make a contribution to the explanation of output growth patterns when changes in the basic factors of production (capital and labour) and simultaneity are taken into account. The same pattern appears in the 1960s, the 1970s, and in the pooled sample, with observable differences in estimated coefficients no greater than might be expected from normal sampling variation. As always in statistical enquiry, these results do not 'prove' anything. They simply show that an appropriately-specified model yields rather robust results which are consistent with the hypothesis that human resource improvements are productivity-augmenting at the aggregate level.[24]

In the other two equations, the measured impact of per capita income growth shows up as expected. A log-interaction term has been included in the nutrition equation to control for a declining calorie demand elasticity as the general nutrition level rises.[25] Note that the endogenous variable in these equations is output growth itself, while population growth enters exogenously. In the system being modelled, percentage change in population is the difference between birth- and death-rates, both defined as 'accumulation parameters'. For the short periods used in estimation, these parameters are assumed to be fixed (determined by the initial levels of several variables, including some of the human resource variables), although it is clear that they can change between periods in a way which makes the model fundamentally recursive.

In the nutrition change equation, the importance of the coefficient of the initial income/nutrition ratio suggests that delayed adjustment is not negligible in explaining current changes in nutrition in LDCs. No major differences in the nutrition equation results for the two decades seem evident. In the literacy equations, however, one important difference is obvious. If the estimates for the 1960s and 1970s are to be believed, they suggest that attempts to move rapidly to mass primary education with limited material and human resources have resulted in a substantial decline in the marginal efficiency of the schooling process in many LDCs. For the 1960s, the estimated probability that any pupil who actually attended primary school would become literate is quite close to one. For the 1970s, however, the probability is apparently lower.[26] This is not to say that rapid expansion has not had a beneficial impact, since 70 per cent of a large number is clearly preferable to 98 per cent of a much smaller number.[27]

There are, of course, numerous possible explanations for this reduction in probability. Its existence seems entirely plausible, however, given the circumstances under which rapid expansion has taken place. In passing, it should be noted that attention was given to the possibility that the literacy probability parameter would itself vary across countries as a function of relative capacity indices such as initial literacy and per capita income. In several trials, no apparent sensitivity emerged, and the assumption of constancy across countries cannot be refuted using the kinds of data which were available for this study.

In summary, it seems fair to conclude that hypothesized impacts for basic education and nutrition on productivity change are consistent with the available data. The growth model performs about equally well for the 1960s and the 1970s. It should be emphasized here that the result for the 1960s lacks one note of ambiguity which is unavoidably present in the second set. The available World Bank estimates for nutritional adequacy and literacy are 'mid-seventies' observations, which can realistically be regarded as random samples from the period 1974-6. Under the assumption that the change registered during the observation period could be extrapolated directly through 1977, these data can be used in an output equation along with measured labour, capital, and output changes for the entire seven-year period. Nevertheless, it is comforting to note the strength of the results for the 1960s.

The results for the life expectancy regression are satisfactory, although this particular equation was subjected to more experimentation than any other in the study. Most plausible variables simply made no contribution to explained variance in the change equation. Both lagged life expectancy change and lagged nutrition change have an apparent impact, along with contemporaneous per capita income change. All the throughput variables previously mentioned appear to make a contribution, as well.[28]

(ii) Testing for outlier effects

Although the reported econometric estimates are the best which could be produced under the circumstances, the reader may feel justified in retaining a certain scepticism concerning the degree to which they actually reflect the hypothesized interactions. Although regression coefficients always purportedly measure 'representative' impacts across data sets which can be characterized by smooth frequency distributions, they may in fact be quite sensitive to the impact of a few outliers in the data. If the term 'outlier' is used rather loosely, it can also represent cases in which purportedly general results are actually reflections of experience in one or two relatively homogeneous subsets of the data. In the current context, for example, it might be imagined that measured human resource impacts were in fact due to particular circumstances in single regions. East Asia has recently been celebrated as an exemplar of both educational and economic progress, and the informed sceptic might well wonder whether the measured impact of literacy on output was not in fact a reflection of a peculiar set of dominating circumstances in East Asia alone.

It is impossible to control for all sources of such scepticism in exercises like the current one. It does seem reasonable, however, to attempt some obvious further tests of the numbers. A simple device is an examination of the scatter diagrams which are associated with the measured partial coefficients in the output equations. In order to produce such scatters, a variable of interest such as literacy change is plotted against 'residualized' output change, where the estimated regression coefficients are used as a means of introducing statistical control for the presence of other variables in the equation. In the following figures, the relevant scatter diagrams are reproduced for literacy and nutrition change for the pooled data. They do not suggest that the measured results have been produced by one or two outliers in either case.

As an additional test for regional dominance in the regression equations, entire regions were excluded from the pooled sample and the system re-estimated in a series of experiments. The results are reported in Figure 3.

Although the exclusion procedure resulted in a substantial loss of degrees of freedom in the cases of Africa and Southern America, the resulting estimates seem to diverge by no more than would be expected from sampling variability. A possible exception is the greater responsiveness of output change to literacy change when Africa is excluded from the sample. In any case, there is certainly nothing in these results to suggest that the estimates for the full pooled sample have been spuriously generated by a dominating association in one region.

One additional source of doubt must be confronted in evaluating the reliability of the results. It is possible to propose explanations for differential growth performance which go considerably beyond those offered by the basic model. It could plausibly be argued that variables such as literacy and nutrition change are in fact rough proxies for other forces whose impact, if directly measured, would render negligible the coefficients of the human resource variables themselves. One extended version of the model has therefore been developed and tested.

FIGURE 2

Literacy and nutrition v. residualized output

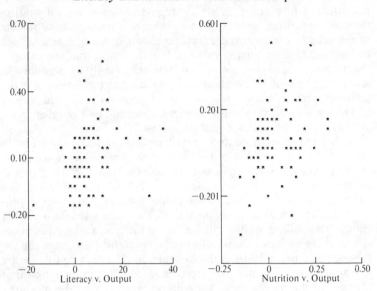

(iii) An open economy variant

It has been suggested by some development theorists that 'extraverted' LDCs can be expected to grow more quickly than others. Many reasons for this have been offered. Countries which subject themselves to the rigours of international competition are quite likely to be forced toward relatively efficient resource allocations, with consequent productivity benefits. At the same time, such economies are the most likely to attract foreign investment, so that the easing of the domestic capital constraint might play a growth-promoting role. Complementary reasons for supposing that extraversion would have a growth-promoting role are easy to imagine. The importing of associated management skills or recent capital vintages could make a measurable difference in aggregate productivity. Similarly, the employment of local labour in efficiently operated export industries might, under normal conditions of turnover, be supposed to have a training impact which would, as it spread, produce more general benefits.

All these arguments are plausible, and many of them have been re-inforced by the performance of several LDCs which have focused on

FIGURE 3
Closed Economy Model with Regional Exclusions

MODEL EQUATIONS

(1) $\langle dq \rangle = [a1 + a2 \star D70] + a3 \star \langle dk \rangle + a4 \star \langle dl \rangle + a5 \star \langle dn \rangle$
$\qquad + a6 \star [E\{t\} - E\{t-1\}]$

(2) $\langle dn \rangle = b1 + [b2 + b3 \star \ln N] \star [\langle dq \rangle - \langle dp \rangle] + b4 \star \ln [(Q/P)/N]$

(3) $E\{t\} - E\{t-1\} \star [1/(1 + \langle da \rangle)] = c1 + c2 \star S \star [\langle da \rangle/(1 + \langle da \rangle)]$
$\qquad + c3 \star [\langle dq \rangle - \langle dp \rangle]$

3SLS RESULTS WITH SPECIFIED REGIONS EXCLUDED (*)

	Africa	*S. America*	*E., S.E. Asia*	*S., S. E. Asia*
a1	.0376 (.0999)	.0149 (.1044)	−.0043 (.0903)	−.0420 (.0949)
a2	−.0574 (.0465)	−.0554 (.0547)	−.0746 (.0444)	−.0594 (.0480)
a3	.1393 (.0271)	.1678 (.0285)	.1706 (.0258)	.1737 (.0267)
a4	.3472 (.2994)	.3957 (.2922)	.4078 (.2334)	.4446 (.2557)
a5	.5475 (.4775)	.5838 (.3971)	.4800 (.3429)	.5934 (.3671)
a6	.0207 (.0056)	.0105 (.0045)	.0099 (.0038)	.0135 (.0041)
b1	−.0514 (.0201)	−.0395 (.0131)	−.0373 (.0144)	−.0427 (.0163)
b2	3.1732 (.8997)	5.6945 (.9562)	3.7803 (1.000)	4.1827 (.9799)
b3	−.6529 (.1919)	−1.2072 (.2064)	−.7965 (.2146)	−.8744 (.2104)
b4	.0419 (.0137)	.0685 (.0169)	.0568 (.0131)	.0481 (.0147)
c1	.6151 (1.7385)	.3658 (1.7556)	1.2819 (1.6770)	.9534 (1.7035)
c2	.8481 (.1009)	.8515 (.1544)	.8387 (.1267)	.8552 (.1317)
c3	9.3233 (2.9056)	8.2971 (3.7554)	5.7916 (3.6345)	7.5153 (3.4090)
OBS	58	58	71	69

(*) Standard errors in parentheses beneath coefficients.

export promotion policies in recent years. East Asian societies such as South Korea, Hong Kong, Taiwan, and Singapore are particularly notable in this regard, of course, although cases in Africa and Latin America can also be cited. In this subsection, a relatively simple extension of the previous modelling exercise will be used to measure the apparent impact of the kinds of factors mentioned above, as well as the degree to which the statistical results for the human resource variables survive the translation to a more complete model.

Again, the specification of the output equation is in growth rates, with the exception of the literacy change variable. In the revised output equation, the relative severity of the foreign exchange constraint is indexed by the contemporaneous growth rate of imports, while a test for any differential effect of manufacturing export performance on productivity is attempted using the growth rate of manufacturing exports. The latter variable is explicitly endogenized in the expanded model.

The manufacturing export equation itself has been specified to reflect some obvious, simple principles of comparative advantage, as well as the simultaneous impact of output growth. Capital is more mobile than labour in the world, and the relative attractiveness of labour as a complement to capital across LDCs must be systematically related to relative quality and price, appropriately measured. In the expanded model, relative wage levels have been represented by per capita incomes, and the available measures of basic education (the literacy rate) and health (life expectancy) have been used as quality indices.[29]

In the open economy model, then, the manufacturing export growth rate in a particular period is specified as a function of the total output growth rate during the period, the initial level of per capita income, and initial levels of literacy and life expectancy. The growth rate of imports is left exogenous. The results for the 1960s and 1970s are reported in Figure 4.

Several interesting patterns are suggested by these results. Certainly, the apparent role of literacy in the growth process is not called into question. Literacy change retains essentially the same magnitude, the appropriate sign, and a high degree of statistical significance in all three sets of regression results. The role of nutrition, on the other hand, is made more ambiguous by the poor result for the 1970s. The use of the import terms in the output equation substantially reduces the directly-estimated contribution of capital. The fact that much capital has been imported by the sample countries makes this result not surprising. With the exception of the nutrition result for the 1970s, then, the use of the open economy model appears to add explanatory power without neutralizing human resource effects on output.

FIGURE 4
Open Economy Model—3SLS Results (*)

POOLED DATA

OBS

$$\langle dq \rangle = .2298 + .0366 \star \langle dk \rangle + .2441 \star \langle dl \rangle + .6194 \star \langle dn \rangle \qquad 71$$
$$(.0963) \ (.0302) \qquad (.2120) \qquad (.4276)$$
$$+ .0091 \star [E\{t\} - E\{t-1\}] + .7257 \star dmx + .1.6080 \star dim$$
$$(.0041) \qquad\qquad (.3429) \qquad (.4538)$$

$$dmx = -.1221 + .0012 \star E + .0024 \star H - .00022 \star (Q/P) + .1955 \star \langle dq \rangle \qquad 71$$
$$(.0951) \ (.00078) \ (.0026) \ (.00007) \qquad (.0434)$$

1960–1970

$$\langle dq \rangle = .1863 + .0060 \star \langle dk \rangle + .2476 \star \langle dl \rangle + 1.5196 \star \langle dn \rangle \qquad 32$$
$$(.1492) \ (.0472) \qquad (.3217) \qquad (.4286)$$
$$+ .0112 \star [E\{t\} - E\{t-1\}] + .6808 \star dmx + 2.6754 \star dim$$
$$(.0045) \qquad\qquad (.4137) \qquad (.9017)$$

$$dmx = .1312 + .0016 \star E - .0048 \star H + .00016 \star (Q/P) + .1951 \star \langle dq \rangle \qquad 32$$
$$(.1493) \ (.0013) \ (.0044) \ (.00014) \qquad (.0616)$$

1970–1977

$$\langle dq \rangle = .0170 + .0780 \star \langle dk \rangle + .4255 \star \langle dl \rangle + .1584 \star \langle dn \rangle \qquad 41$$
$$(.0583) \ (.0343) \qquad (.2540) \qquad (.3256)$$
$$+ .0089 \star [E\{t\} - E\{t-1\}] + .7661 \star dmx + 1.000 \star dim$$
$$(.0031) \qquad\qquad (.1745) \qquad (.3362)$$

$$dmx = -.3011 + .0014 \star E + .0064 \star H - .00038 \star (Q/P) + .1672 \star \langle dq \rangle \qquad 41$$
$$(.0924) \ (.00074) \ (.0024) \ (.00006) \qquad (.0523)$$

VARIABLES NOT PREVIOUSLY DEFINED
dmx = Growth rate of manufacturing exports
dim = Growth rate of imports

(*) Standard errors in parentheses beneath coefficients. The estimates for the nutrition and literacy equations are effectively identical to those obtained for the closed economy model. These results have been excluded from the Figure for the sake of readability.

Even a cursory examination of the manufacturing equation results reveals that the fit is much better for the 1970s than for the previous decade. As always, two alternative explanations for this result are possible. The first might suggest that one of the two sets of results is simply a sampling accident, and that the export equation is: (a) irrelevant or (b) acceptable, depending upon the predisposition of the observer. A second plausible interpretation of the result might be that the world has changed, and that the international market is now sufficiently articulated for these simple measures of comparative advantage in labour resources to capture an important source of differential competitiveness for LDCs.

If the optimistic interpretation of the mixed result is accepted, an interesting implication for human resource policy follows immediately. If it is really true that manufacturing export activity is a source of differential productivity gain, for whatever reason, and if it is also true that part of the comparative advantage is attributable to basic human resources such as literacy, then it follows that countries which pay little attention to these factors will suffer a double penalty. They will lose part of the output differential which is apparent in both sets of results on 'closed economy' grounds alone. In addition, they will experience more difficulty in export expansion, with its attendant benefits, than their counterparts which have focused on human resources. If the pooled results are regarded as the best summary of the evidence from both decades, the role of education in this domain certainly shows up more convincingly than the role of health (in so far as health is indexed by life expectancy).

Obviously, this sort of argument is only partial. Funds for human resource investments and the support of heavy associated recurrent costs may well come from surpluses which could be allocated to physical investments. To say that human resource investments can have benefits is not, therefore, the same thing as claiming that the productivity impact of these investments is necessarily superior to that of physical investment. At this point, an explicit consideration of the trade-off question would be premature. After the entire socio-economic growth model has been specified and fitted to the available data, the resulting equations will be combined into a simulation model which will provide a vehicle for trade-off exercises.

(iv) The investment rate

Before moving from a consideration of output components in the growth model to the demographic side, some attention must be paid to the investment rate. A recursive specification of its relationship with the rest of the output equations seems justifiable. It is the level of the investment rate which determines the change in the capital stock and subsequent change in the output growth rate. Since the investment rate is itself hypothesized to be a function of several variables which represent initial conditions in any growth period, the investment equation has been estimated separately by ordinary least squares.

In many ways, the investment relation represents the most limited part of this study. It is obvious that the observable aggregate investment rate in any society results from the interplay of many public and private resource allocation decisions. In addition, both domestic and international factors can play a role. No attempt has been made to handle these complexities in a structural model. Rather, the equation which is fitted to the data is a reduced form with some rather heroic presuppositions built in.

The basic investment equation has three components. These components are all determinants of the supply of investible funds, and an implicit assumption is made that this supply is actually translated into investment activity through the intermediation of public or private institutions. As any analyst of financial affairs in LDCs can affirm, this view is an oversimplification at best. At least, however, one would expect a substantial degree of correlation between the supply of investible funds and investment activity across countries.

The supply-side components which are incorporated into the investment equation for this exercise are three in number. Per capita income is included, since it is to be anticipated that the rate of personal savings will rise as a society moves away from the subsistence margin. In addition, two human resource variables are incorporated in the specification. Life expectancy is employed because of an hypothesized link between expected lifespan and savings behaviour on the part of individuals in a particular society. In effect this represents nothing more than an extension of the life-cycle approach to savings behaviour. The literacy rate is included to test the hypothesis that higher levels of basic education promote a fundamental change in attitude toward economic calculation and long-range planning. In the view of some, this effect may be particularly pronounced in rural areas.

Again, then, all the incorporated variables are really supply-side factors, and the explicit connection between the associated forces and the ultimate realized investment rate is left obscure in the specification. It should be noted in passing that both basic education and health could be regarded as human capital variables, in the spirit of the manufacturing export equations, and that an alternative interpretation of any perceived effect on the investment rate would pass through the impact of differences in human capital on the international flow of investment. Whether the hypothesized effect is foreign, domestic, or some combination, however, the investment equation remains entirely a supply-side construct.

With all this as precautionary introduction, we now pass to a brief consideration of specification and estimation.[30] In this case, as in the others, the regression equation has been fitted to changes in the investment rate rather than to levels. The right-hand side has been made explicitly non-linear in an attempt to control for a presumed decrease in the marginal impact of the included supply factors as the investment rate rises. Thus, changes in life expectancy and the literacy rate are divided by the initial investment rate in the complete specification, while shifts in per capita income are specified as percentage changes rather than absolute differences.

The estimation results, as produced by least-squares regression, are reproduced in Figure 4a. The initial investment rate was also incorporated as a means of controlling for any sensitivity of autonomous shift factors to initial conditions. The scatter diagram in Figure 4a suggests that the relationship between investment level in 1960 and changes in investment from 1960 to 1977 has been strongly characterized by regression toward the mean. The scatter shows that (ceteris paribus), countries with unusually high investment rates exhibited a

FIGURE 4a
Investment Rate Change (1960-77)

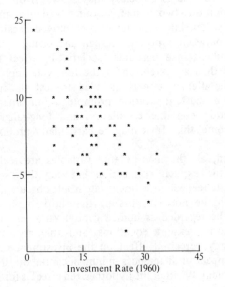

Investment Rate (1960)

FIGURE 5
Investment Rate Changes, 1960-1977 (*)

	OBS	R**2

$$I\{t\} - I\{t-1\} = 11.0502 - .7842 \star I\{t-1\}$$
$$(2.4479) \quad (.1351)$$

OBS 39   R**2 .63

$$+ 5.3056 \star [Q/P\{t\} - Q/P\{t-1\}]/[Q/P\{t-1\}]$$
$$(1.6174)$$

$$+ 3.1372 \star [E\{t\} - E\{t-1\}]/I\{t-1\}$$
$$(1.3612)$$

$$I\{t\} - I\{t-1\} = 8.1247 - .5321 \star I\{t-1\}$$
$$(3.3318) \quad (.1524)$$

OBS 58   R**2 .59

$$+ 6.2889 \star [Q/P\{t\} - Q/P\{t-1\}/[Q/P\{t-1\}]$$
$$(1.1106)$$

$$+ 3.6924 \star [H\{t\} - H\{t-1\}]/I\{t-1\}$$
$$(1.7719)$$

$$I\{t\} - I\{t-1\} = 8.3445 - .6939 \star I\{t-1\}$$
$$(6.9651) \quad (.2568)$$

OBS 39   R**2 .62

$$+ 5.3017 \star [Q/P\{t\} - Q/P\{t-1\}]/[Q/P\{t-1\}]$$
$$(1.6369)$$

$$+ 2.1829 \star [H\{t\} - H\{t-1\}]/I\{t-1\}$$
$$(5.2518)$$

$$+ 3.0705 \star [E\{t\} - E\{t-1\}]/I\{t-1\}$$
$$(1.3869)$$

VARIABLES NOT PREVIOUSLY DEFINED
I = Investment rate

(*) Standard errors in parentheses beneath coefficients.

decline over the period, while countries with unusually low rates exhibited an increase.

The regression equation in this case has been fitted to seventeen-year changes in order to reduce the effect of measurement error and sluggish responsiveness on the overall measure of error variance. The results are in Figure 5.

The results suggest an important role for income change in the generation of investment rate change, and changes in the literacy rate have apparently had an impact as well. Although its effect is not statistically significant when it is incorporated along with literacy in the equation, life expectancy change emerges impressively when literacy change is excluded. The literacy data are relatively sparse, and it should be noted that twenty degress of freedom have been gained in the second equation. A fundamental ambiguity therefore remains. It is possible that multicollinearity is the culprit, but it also entirely possible that life expectancy change has no independent explanatory power.

As a conclusion to this section, it is worth noting that the use of seventeen-year changes in estimation throws the recursive assumption into doubt. Over this long a period, a rising investment rate would undoubtedly promote upward shifts in human resource variables, so that simultaneous causation (in a rather complex, second-order form) would create difficulties for the interpretation of regression coefficients. Although the long-period results will be used in subsequent simulation exercises, the possibility of some simultaneity bias in the coefficients of this particular equation must be borne in mind. Let us hope that future work can cast further light on this entire subject by recasting investment rate determination into explicitly structural form with allowances made for the contributions of public and private decision makers (both domestic and foreign), as well as the supply-side variables which have been utilized here.

(v) Unsuccessful experiments

No econometric study ever proceeds from start to finish in the clean, precise way suggested by the textbooks. In the consideration of behaviour in any socio-economic system, there are always many hypotheses which compete in the mind of the researcher. When the research effort involves substantial discussion with others who can themselves suggest many plausible and ingenious ideas (and this was certainly the case in the current effort), the competitive field becomes crowded indeed.

Under these circumstances, the econometrician must contend with two substantial sources of uncertainty in the research process. The first is the problem of equation specification. While standard economic production functions have been much studied and the properties of contending specifications are pretty well understood, the same cannot be said of the functions which 'produce' life expectancy or literacy in a society. For that matter, the simultaneous specification of output and social indicators is itself relatively unconventional, and existing work provides little prior guidance concerning the appropriate specification of combined production functions.

Thus, experimentation with alternative functional forms becomes an inevitable part of undertakings like the present one. Much experimentation of this kind lies behind the results which are presented here, although Occam's razor was applied in most cases when the temptation to venture into truly exotic specifications became strong. Basically, my concern has been to work with cross-section changes rather than cross-section levels, for reasons which have already been discussed in detail. In most cases, then, attention has been confined to the competition between percentage changes and absolute changes. There are problems with either measure, but consistent specification moved the proceedings toward percentage changes in the response block.

It should be re-emphasized that the main difference between percentage and absolute change specifications lies in the underlying assumption concerning the degree to which right-hand side variables are substitutable for one another in determining outcomes. A specification in absolute changes asserts that right-hand side variables are perfect substitutes in the process, while the use of percentage changes is equivalent to asserting that the variables are 'very good' (unit-elastic) but not perfect substitutes.

It is, of course, entirely possible that neither assumption is appropriate. In using asymptote-modified forms of relations in the accumulation and response specifications, I have moved away from these simple forms, but toward specifications whose properties have not been completely thought through at this point. This kind of thinking needs to be done, but it is a separate project in itself. It certainly deserves an entry in the category 'Priority for Future Research'.

There is, of course, a second source of uncertainty in this kind of study which interacts with the first one. In each of the processes which were examined, the explanatory power of many seemingly-plausible variables turned out to be negligible. 'Negligible' is a loaded term in econometrics, of course, since some variable which theoretically has a role to play should not be excluded from an equation just because the standard error of its coefficient is relatively large in a particular sample result. Econometric art definitely merges with science in this particular domain, since the intersection of available data shrinks with the inclusion of more and more variables in a model. In cross-section work on a relatively limited sample, the fundamental discipline imposed by the degrees-of-freedom problem is severe.

Although the final results represent equations fitted using variables which seem to 'work', it is certainly important to mention the also-rans as well. Sherlock Holmes's dictum concerning the dog which didn't bark is as important in this kind of detective work as in any other. In the interests of comprehensibility, our gallery of failures will be presented sequentially.

In the output equation, there has actually been remarkably little evolution. The one major exception is provided by a series of experiments with life expectancy, all of which failed to provide any evidence of a direct link between contemporaneous life expectancy change and output change. This was somewhat surprising, since previous work on the 1960s which I had undertaken did suggest an important role for life expectancy change.[31] For the seventies, this materialized neither in percentage nor in absolute change specifications. It is true, of course, that the initial level of life expectancy seems to have an impact through its effect on the growth in exports of manufactures (in the 1970s, at least), but no change relation can be discerned. This presents one of the more interesting puzzles to emerge from the modelling exercise. Since the model's results for the 1960s and 1970s are similar in many other respects, why not in this one? Perhaps the result for the 1960s was spurious, and perhaps not. In any case, this problem remains to be resolved.

The other major set of experiments performed on the output equation involved the comparison of the performance of published labour force growth data with the performance of adult population change as a proxy. As previously mentioned, few would argue with the contention that the adult data are more carefully collected. Over short periods, labour force participation and unemployment rates must come very close to being constant multipliers, and they should therefore wash out when percentage changes are employed. In any case, the experiments certainly seemed to go in favour of the adult data. Estimates based on the labour force data were very unstable from sample to sample, and they frequently yielded estimated elasticities so large as to be very unreasonable. The estimates obtained with the adult population growth rate, on the other hand, are quite stable from sample to sample and very reasonable.

Like the output equation, the nutrition equation has not been the object of a tremendous amount of experimentation. Absolute changes have been tried, but they do worse than percentage changes. (This is also true for the contribution of nutrition change in the output change equation, so the percentage change specification has no competition in this case.)

The literacy equation has been subjected to two experiments which were not fruitful. There is a plausible argument which asserts that self-education should be positively related to life expectancy as well as per capita income, and various specifications of life-expectancy change were duly tried. None worked. In addition, it seemed plausible to suppose that the literacy-production-probability coefficient would be sensitive to existing levels of per capita income, health, and literacy in different societies. The appropriate experiments with interaction terms were undertaken, and all the results were robustly insignificant.

In the case of the health equation, the present product is the result of very substantial experimentation. When life expectancy change is measured in percentage terms, it is necessary to introduce some control for asymptotic behaviour on the right-hand side of the equation. If such a term is not included, sadly enough, an absolutely beautiful life expectancy change equation emerges. In this fragile but exquisite construct, seemingly important roles emerge for almost every variable which might plausibly be supposed to have an impact on life expectancy change. Present and lagged changes in medical personnel, present and lagged changes in nutrition, present and lagged changes in schooling— all show up strongly, with seeming significance, and with correctly descending lag weights in every case. Unfortunately, the whole thing is totally non-robust. With the common-sense introduction of a simple hyperbolic term $(1/H)$ to control for asymptotic behaviour, the structure collapses and only lagged nutrition emerges from the rubble.

Now, there are two possible responses to a situation such as the one just described. One plausible argument would hold that structural explanations are better than non-structural explanations, and that if the choice is between a set of plausible explanatory variables and a simple hyperbolic term the former should be chosen. One the other hand, when this simple term 'explains' as much variation in the data as a whole host of contenders, Occam's razor comes readily to mind. In this case, the flowery construct has been suppressed because it is so non-robust. The variables which remain in the equation, on the other hand, are very resistant to specification change, and their presence has been justified in detail in the text. In passing, it should also be noted that several other plausible variables were tried in the life expectancy equation, and none of them had any apparent impact. Present and past changes in population per hospital bed and population per 'nursing person' (a vaguely-defined concept at best) failed to produce any meaningful results, as did the initial levels of the same variables. In addition, the available measure of 'safe water' availability had no effect.

In the manufacturing export equation, very little experimentation has been done. All of the variables in the equation seemed plausible, given the argument about human resources which formed the basis for this exercise and the evident importance of relative wages in a competitive environment. The bad result for the 1960s introduces a major ambiguity, of course.

We now pass to the investment rate equation, which was not the subject of many experiments other than those already reported. The one exception involved a plausible argument about the role of 'extraversion' of the economy in the determination of the investment rate. It was hypothesized that a change in the ratio of exports to GDP should elicit some response in the investment rate, on the theory that large enterprises (public or private) are disproportionately involved in trading activities and find it easier to mobilize savings. Although the export-ratio term generally had the correct sign in the investment rate change equations when it was included, the associated standard error was always quite large. This variable was therefore excluded from the final estimates.

PART II

HUMAN RESOURCES AND
POPULATION GROWTH

CHAPTER 4

FERTILITY CHANGE

Although per capita income is frequently employed as an index of 'development' for LDCs, it is arguable that life expectancy at birth is a better measure of the quality of life. Most income distributions are approximately log-normal, so that the estimated mean income for a society can mask widespread poverty. Since none of us enjoys many more than four score years, however, mean life expectancy is a dependable aggregate measure. It has the additional virtue of perfect comparability across countries, while per capita income comparisons are plagued by index number problems. Let us adopt life expectancy as a rough index of development, then, and look at three instructive pictures. They are scatter diagrams showing the relationship between life expectancy and the general fertility rate for LDCs in 1960, 1970, and 1977.

If these three pictures (displayed in Figure 6) are viewed as snapshots, it is difficult to avoid the feeling that all societies are flowing over the same waterfall as time passes.[32] Note that as the minimum life expectancy in the set increases during the two decades, fewer and fewer countries are upstream from the falls. The point at which the plunge begins (50–55 years) seems to be relatively constant.

If life expectancy is accepted as an index of development, we can state an obvious proposition: development has something to do with fertility decline. Unfortunately, this is probably the only proposition which would command general assent from the community of demographers and population economists at present. As an introduction to this discussion of fertility change, I can do no better than quote from a recent paper by Berelson, Mauldin, and Segal (1979):

The theoretical position of the 'basic determinants' of fertility appears to be in considerable disarray: On the one hand, the received wisdom from traditional demographic transition theory is increasingly challenged and qualified as more becomes known; on the other hand the offered reformulations are not yet widely accepted. Everything is always 'more complicated than that.'

(i) Some contending fertility theories

Among economists, there wasn't much faith in the Demographic Transition to begin with. From the theorist's perspective, Leibenstein

FIGURE 6
Life Expectancy (X) v. Fertility (Y)

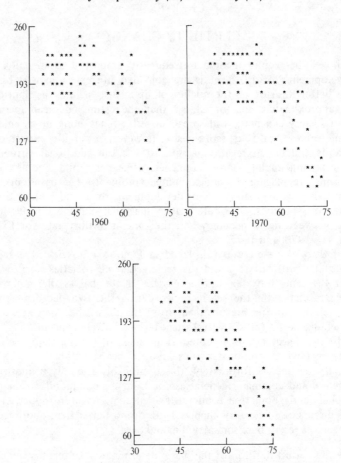

has noted '. . . [the Transition] seems like a grand historical generalization buttressed by a variety of *ad hoc* causal assertions.'[33] Among
demographers, faith has also been eroded as detailed historical research
has accumulated. Although these studies have revealed numerous anoma-
lies which call the Transition into question, they have not been prin-
cipally concerned with producing a new general theory.[34]

As the faith has waned, researchers have scattered themselves across the scholarly landscape. Some demographers with a particular interest in LDCs have devoted themselves to expanding the fund of information available. At the cross-national level, the knowledge, attitude and practice (KAP) studies of the 1960s and the World Fertility Survey have made major contributions to the data base.[35] Intensive field research at the village level has also proceeded, with particular emphasis on measurement of the economic benefits and costs of children and the impact of village institutions on fertility behaviour.[36] In a general sense, these LDC-focused efforts replicate the European studies: the national efforts do not produce data sufficient for unambiguous structural analysis; the village studies are expensive and therefore sparse, although they produce valuable insights concerning structural determinants of fertility.

While much effort has gone into intensive data collection during the past decade, some scholars have worked on new theories of fertility determination with the aid of existing data. Paradoxically, the most influential work by economists has been done by a group with head-quarters at Chicago and Columbia who have seldom studied develop-ment problems. Their 'new household economics' applies microeconomic theory to forms of behaviour whose analysis has traditionally been ceded to other social scientists.[37] Among their activities has been the formulation of a theory of family fertility behaviour. Families are assumed to allocate resources (including their members' time) so as to maximize a common utility function which includes the quantity and 'quality' of children. Since both quantity and quality are superior goods, richer families will have fewer children if there is a dispropor-tionate rise in opportunity costs as income increases.[38]

This theory of fertility determination has been marketed quite aggressively by its proponents. Leibenstein (1974) has aptly sum-marized a common reaction among demographers:

To some of those who had been laboring in the vineyards of demo-graphy for decades, the efforts of economists in the sixties and seventies to develop a theory of fertility must have appeared like the invasion of a horde of primitives on a technologically advanced community pro-claiming loudly their intent to reinvent the wheel . . . One can under-stand the disdain of some demographers for these efforts, some of which suggested that the economist in question had not bothered to assimilate very much of the earlier findings. (p. 458.)

Other economists, among whom Leibenstein is probably the best known, have paid more attention to the mainstream of demographic thought while preserving important elements of the Chicago approach. The difference lies in the relative importance assigned to social and

institutional factors in determining tastes and patterns of behaviour.
'Socio-economic' models of fertility determination characteristically
attempt to combine these variables with economic factors to explain
the desire for children, the nature of fertility control attempts, and
infant survival rates.[39]

The socio-economic tradition in demographic analysis bridges the
gap between the Chicago approach and an analysis which might be
termed the 'proximate determinants' approach. In this structuralist
view, fertility is the outcome of a social process rather than the result
of an explicit decision. Institutional, social, and economic factors
determine at least four proximate determinants of fertility: female
age at marriage, prevalence of induced abortion, use of contraceptives,
and the duration of natural contraception during lactation. An appropriate structural model includes separate equations for each proximate
determinant. Taken together, these factors in turn should explain
almost all of the observed international variance in fertility levels.[40]

Along with the structuralist, socio-economic, and micro-economic
approaches mentioned above, there is also a 'psycho-political' variant
which is worthy of note. In a sense, this approach implies further
disaggregation of all the other approaches. The essence is the notion
that family decisions and responses to environmental factors are not
conditioned by one uniform set of values. Rather, the family itself
is an arena in which individual members' interests are in continual
interplay and conflict. General parameters of 'family behaviour' estimated in either Chicago-type or proximate determinants models are
not true structural parameters, in this view. Rather, they are averages
which reflect the balance of family power at any point in time. A
truly structural model would have two stages: (1) The determination
of desired fertility outcomes for different family members; (2) The
determination of value dominance in the politics of family relations.[41]

(ii) A predictive fertility equation

This brief survey of the theoretical terrain suggests that some of the
controversy may have been unnecessarily heated. Ultimately, it is
difficult to detect any real conflict between the existing schools of
thought. The Chicago approach is silent concerning the way in which
a family's utility function and perception of opportunity cost are
fashioned. Thus, the micro-economists' behavioural 'parameters'
could reflect the outcome of intra-familial conflict. Individuals and
families exist in a social and institutional environment, so it is undeniably true that their surroundings play a role in setting their tastes
and perceived opportunity costs. The proximate determinants could

be regarded as fertility 'inputs' which are themselves 'produced' by numerous factors. It should be possible to specify a two-level production model which preserves some independent status for fertility as a decision variable.

Since the existing approaches seem more complementary than contradictory, it is probable that any new General Theory of fertility determination will incorporate them all. In the meantime, my own feeling is that the absence of a consensus does not fatally hinder the construction of a predictive fertility equation. My argument depends on two propositions: first, that a cross-section international model of fertility change may well yield better long-run predictions than those obtainable from large country-specific data sets (even if they were available for LDCs, which is not the case); secondly, that the use of international data forces the adoption of a predictive equation whose level of aggregation makes it almost a common reduced form for all the behavioural models which have been proposed.

The first proposition is based on a standard problem of extrapolation in econometrics. Suppose that we want to forecast long-run demographic change for a particular country. If we fit a model only to historical data for that country, we will not have incorporated any information about reactions to new circumstances. In any econometric equation, the error variance in prediction grows as the predictive values of right-hand variables move away from their historical means.[42] Thus, we can anticipate huge prediction error at the outer limit of a long-range forecast.

We have only two hopes for extricating ourselves from this dilemma. The first hope lies in the fact that national development improves the circumstances of some people before it touches the lives of others. Econometric analysis of the behaviour of the 'advanced' group may therefore be used as a guide to the future behaviour of other groups as their circumstances change.

Some reflection, unfortunately, suggests that this approach is no panacea. In a poor LDC, there may not be sufficient contemporary variation in variables such as life expectancy to support this kind of extrapolation. Even if there is substantial variation, it may well have existed for only one generation. For phenomena such as fertility, adjustment to changed circumstances may take as long as a generation. Thus the current behaviour of advantaged groups in LDCs may not be a reliable guide to their behaviour a generation hence, even if their circumstances do not change further.

If either or both of these reservations are seriously acknowledged, then it is sensible to consider the second hope: incorporation of behavioural variation through international comparison. The idea that the future for a country in Africa can be discerned in contemporary Central America has its own drawbacks, of course. In this book, I am obviously betting that cross country comparisons add a meaningful dimension to the analysis of fertility change (and all the other changes, for that matter).

Now we come to the second proposition which was stated on page 49. For international cross-section estimation, a predictive fertility equation is necessarily a reduced form. Since this reduced form is about the same for aggregated versions of all the available theoretical models, the selection of appropriate variables is not a very controversial task. It should be noted that the parameters of a reduced-form equation are combinations of the structural equation parameters. The reduced form is therefore perfectly acceptable for prediction, even if it is consistent with several structural explanation systems.

We can roughly categorize the reduced-form variables as belonging to the 'demand side' or the 'supply side' of fertility determination. As Birdsall (1980) has noted, past econometric work on fertility has been limited to a consideration of variables which condition the desire for children because of the lack of data on available contraceptives and family planning services.[43] This necessary concentration only on the demand side has always entailed the risk of serious specification bias in the estimated parameter values.[44] I was fortunate enough to undertake this study during a period when a comprehensive 'supply side' variable became available for the first time. I hope that this chapter can make some contribution to the fertility debate by presenting balanced estimates. As previously noted, I have also confined my attention to a model specified purely in changes, so that some of the interpretive ambiguity associated with cross-section work has been removed.

(iii) Selection of variables: the demand side

For reasons which have been discussed in Chapter 1 and which should have been further illuminated by my survey in section (i), at least three variables should be included in any reduced-form fertility equation: income, education, and the infant mortality rate. The appropriateness of female age at marriage as a reduced-form variable is a little more controversial.[45] In the Chicago approach, age at marriage and fertility should be determined in two separate equations derived from the first order conditions for full utility maximization. In the other theories, however, age at marriage could legitimately be considered a causal variable in the system. Thus, the inclusion of age at marriage as a reduced-form variable would have a modest theoretical implication, and a statistical test of its significance would be of some independent interest.[46]

There are, of course, other variables which have been proposed as determinants of cohort-specific fertility rates: urbanization, the income distribution, and the status of women, to name but a few. I have not been able to use these variables because the data are so poor. In any case, I doubt whether the exclusion of indices of urbanization and the distribution of income would be very damaging even if good data were available. With respect to the use of 'urbanization' as a causal variable, Birdsall (1980) concludes a review of the existing evidence by stating: '. . . there is no real evidence that residence in an urban area *per se* reduces fertility' (p. 52). In some societies, urban residence may be a prerequisite for access to amenities which affect fertility decline: education, income and the improved levels of sanitation and health care which cause declines in infant mortality. In an equation which controls for these effects directly, the exclusion of urbanization should not be particularly damaging.

The 'distribution of income' is frequently cited as another important determinant of national aggregate fertility rates, but its role must be interpreted carefully.[47] Existing time series work for particular countries (e.g. Dyson *et al.* (1978)) has repeatedly suggested that the rate of fertility decline decreases as family income increases. Thus, at a given level of mean income, any transfer of income from the rich to the poor will generate a lower aggregate fertility rate. There is nothing in this argument which says that the share of the poor *per se* is an important variable. In the final analysis, it is still income levels for individual families which have an effect. The essential quarrel with the use of mean (or per capita) income as an aggregate proxy for income status in a population is that there can be very large variance in the distribution (and therefore in aggregate fertility) at any level of per capita income.

It seems to me that the fundamental thrust of this argument is advocacy of the median rather than the mean as a summary measure of family income in particular countries. Since median measures are generally not available, the mean is frequently used as a proxy. We can therefore regard use of mean income in a cross-section regression as a classic errors-in-variables problem. In general, the result should be a biased estimate of the impact of median income on fertility. The severity of the bias depends on the size of the measurement error variance. With actual data on the distribution of income available, the median could in fact be approximated and the problem largely avoided.

There are two main reasons why I have not used income distribution estimates in my fertility equation. Both are derived from the fact that the equation is estimated on changes rather than levels. The first, as I have mentioned, is purely practical: good income distribution data for LDCs in 1960 are practically non-existent, and to include change in income distribution as a right-hand variable would be to condemn myself to a fatal loss of degrees of freedom.

The second reason is theoretical. Beyond the point where fertility is at its maximum level, it seems reasonable to specify the relationship between income and fertility as log-linear: that is, fertility decline is less steep with each income increment. In a simple bivariate model, we have:

(10) $F\{t\} = a0 + a1 \star \log [Y\{t\}]$

The time derivative of (10) is:

(11) $dF/dt = [a1/Y] \star [dY/dt] = a1 \star \langle dy \rangle$

Thus, the dynamic equivalent of the log-linear model is an equation which relates change in the fertility rate to percentage change in income. This result is fortuitous, since it suggests that the errors-in-variables problem associated with the use of per capita income is much less severe when time changes are employed.

The reason lies in the tenacity of prevailing income distributions. Careful work by economic historians has suggested that Western income distributions have remained relatively stable over many decades. Except for truly revolutionary upheavals, it is plausible to suppose that the same rough stability has characterized LDCs. If we adopt the assumption that all family incomes in a society remain fixed multiples of the lowest income, then the percentage change in mean income will be the same as the percentage change of all incomes, including that of the median family.

In reality, of course, income distributions change (or at least fluctuate) somewhat through time. No one could seriously argue, however, that the variance in distributional changes across LDCs during relatively short periods has been greater than the variance in their income distributions. The implication is clear: a theoretical model whose dynamic form relates change in fertility to percentage change in mean income is less subject to the errors-in-variables problem than its static counterpart. Thus, percentage change in mean income (which is observable) can serve as a good proxy for percentage change in median income (which is not).

The final variable mentioned above—women's status—is unquestionably important. However, it is multi-faceted, the facets are difficult to index, and the relevant data are largely unavailable. The only exception is the female literacy rate, for which some data have become available in recent years. Adequate time series, however, are impossible to find. The exclusion of any measure of female status is therefore largely a matter of necessity.

(iv) Selection of variables: the supply side

Mauldin and Lapham have recently devised an international index of family planning activity after a detailed study of the experiences of many LDCs. Besides paying considerable attention to 'appropriate education', this index is designed to give weight to institutional capacity, public support, and the provision of contraceptives. Although its scoring system is undoubtedly rather arbitrary in some respects, it is at least an attempt to quantify a complex phenomenon. I have employed it as the 'supply side' variable in my fertility equation.[48]

It should be noted that the Mauldin–Berelson index is not immune to the danger associated with the construction of any such performance measure: it is difficult to be objective about relative family planning effort when observations on performance have already been made. Thus, there is some risk that the Mauldin–Berelson index is actually a 'residual'. In addition, this index may measure a phenomenon which is determined simultaneously with the fertility rate. If it is true that enhanced family planning effort should yield some observable benefits over time, it may also be true that such efforts are only likely to become important in countries where the circumstances appear encouraging on other grounds. An explicitly simultaneous specification therefore seems advisable, and a separate equation explaining variations in planning activity should be specified as well.

Since it is desirable to estimate the fertility equation in time-difference form, the Mauldin–Berelson index introduces an additional complication. It is reasonable to suppose that all countries in the set would have received a score near zero on this index in 1960. However, the same assumption would by no means be justified for 1970. Thus, the use of the M–B index forces a seventeen-year specification in changes. This form may well be reasonable on other grounds, since adjustments to changes in other model variables will certainly not be instantaneous. In addition, the use of a relatively long time-interval should aid in reducing the relative effect of measurement error on regression results.

(v) The incorporation of age cohort effects

As noted in Chapter 1, any consideration of fertility rates would be incomplete without an attempt to incorporate the impact of differential age cohort proportions across countries. In this study, three alternative specifications of cohort-specific variability have been evaluated econometrically. Although the mathematical details and the extended discussion of results have been relegated to Appendix B, the essence of the modelling approach and the final estimation results will be presented and discussed here.

It can be argued that all of the factors mentioned above should have some impact on the fertility rate of any female age cohort in a particular society. The scarcity of appropriate data, however, has prevented detailed econometric work on the degree to which the impacts differ across cohorts. In this study, an attempt has been made to approach the question as a set of specific hypotheses which can be tested econometrically.

Basically, the statistical 'foil' employed is a model which allows variables to have different marginal impacts on the behaviour of different age cohorts. With limited degrees of freedom it is difficult to incorporate more than a few such cohorts, and here the relevant female age group (taken to be in the range 15-49) has been divided into three subgroups (15-24, 25-34, and 35-49). The model in which all marginal impacts are allowed to vary by age cohort has been used as the basis for testing a substantially constrained model in which marginal impacts are identical across cohorts but cohort-specific rates themselves are allowed to differ by a constant term. The test establishes that the equality constraints cannot be rejected, and Occam's razor has been employed in the choice of fertility rate model. In the final specification, the imposition of the marginal equality constraints generates a model in which simple differences in age cohort percentages enter additively along with the variables previously mentioned.

CHAPTER 5

ECONOMETRIC RESULTS

(i) The role of age at marriage

As noted in Chapter 4, a test of the significance of female age at marriage in a reduced-form fertility equation has some theoretical interest. Unfortunately, data on singulate age at marriage (SAM) across countries are quite scarce at the present time.[49] Since this study focuses on changes rather than levels, the scarcity problem is compounded. It has not been possible to incorporate age at marriage into the fertility change equation without reducing degrees of freedom to absurdly low levels. However, the possible effect of this variable on fertility has been considered sufficiently important to warrant an independent look in cross-section. Figure 7 reports a set of regression results which have been used to evaluate the apparent impact of age at marriage. The particular nature of the Mauldin–Berelson index has allowed data pooling only for the years 1960 and 1977. In all regression equations, the constrained linear specification of age cohort impact has been employed.

As a prelude to the discussion of these results, I stress that they do not in any sense constitute a test of the proximate determinants model of fertility. Since the proximate determinants are essential intermediaries in the process of fertility control, they have a rightful place in any fully-specified structural model. I am working here with a fertility equation which is essentially a reduced form. SAM can only account for unexplained variance in this equation if it is significantly affected by excluded variables which are not highly correlated with those in the reduced form. In a sense, then, these results give some insight into the completeness of the reduced form which I have adopted.

The first regression equation represents a simple model of SAM determination. Life expectancy and education (proxy supplied by literacy) are specified as causal variables. It is quite plausible to suppose that people will choose to marry later if they can expect to live longer. The reasoning underlying this hypothesis resembles the life-cycle interpretation of consumption and savings behaviour. The experience of more advanced economies suggests a significant tendency to defer marriage for investment in education, coupled with an apparent desire to postpone family responsibilities until later in life. The regression results are resoundingly consistent with this hypothesis. The estimated coefficient for life expectancy suggests a high degree of responsiveness,

FIGURE 7

Cross-section Results:
Singulate Age at Marriage, Human Resource Variables,
and Fertility Rate Differentials (*)

(POOLED DATA, 1960 and 1977)

			OBS	R**2

(1) $SAM = 8.756 + .210 \star H + .011 \star E$ 45   .64
     (1.298) (.025)   (.008)

(2) $F = -213.51 + 492.29 \star W1524 + 701.20 \star W2534$ 40   .76
    (137.80) (138.01)   (268.80)

        $-2.62 \star PLAN + 10.40 \star D - .288 \star D \star\star 2 - 3.93 \star SAM$
         (.89)   (3.41)   (.096)   (2.26)

(3) $F = -206.95 + 483.23 \star W1524 + 691.12 \star W2534$ 40   .75
    (142.17) (144.47)   (275.56)

        $-2.63 \star PLAN + 10.30 \star D - .286 \star D \star\star 2$
         (.90)   (3.48)   (.097)

        $- 3.78 \star SAM - .0076 \star Q/P$
       (2.37)   (.030)

(4) $F = -185.11 + 411.25 \star W1524 + 608.06 \star W2534$ 37   .80
    (131.26) (132.74)   (256.40)

        $-2.52 \star PLAN + 10.55 \star D - .309 \star D \star\star 2$
         (.92)   (3.53)   (.094)

        $-1.04 \star SAM - .521 \star E$
       (2.51)   (.27)

VARIABLES NOT FORMERLY DEFINED

SAM	=	Female singulate mean age at marriage
F	=	Fertility rate
$W1524$	=	Women in age cohort 15–24 as a percentage of all women in age cohort 15–49
$W2534$	=	Women in age cohort 25–34 (as a percentage . . .)
D	=	Death rate
H	=	Life expectancy
Q/P	=	Per capita income
$PLAN$	=	Mauldin–Berelson index of family planning activity

(*) Standard errors in parentheses beneath coefficients. For the sake of consistency, all econometric work for this study has avoided the inclusion of the major oil-producing countries. With both literacy and SAM in use, however, degrees of freedom are at a premium. In this case, an exception to the general rule seems warranted.

and the confidence interval around the estimate is obviously quite narrow. Since it was supposed that education might play a role which could be distinguished from that of life expectancy, literacy was also included as an explanatory variable. The literacy result is considerably weaker, although the suggested level of responsiveness is again fairly high. When per capita income is considered along with literacy and life expectancy, it explains no additional variance in age at marriage. Both literacy and life expectancy, on the other hand, retain the approximate levels of association suggested by the two-variable regression.

The first regression result suggests that a substantial component of the variance in SAM is accounted for by variables which are already in the reduced-form fertility equation. Education enters the equation directly. Life expectancy is essentially the dual of the death rate, which is also in the fertility equation. It remains to be seen, then, whether there are exogenous variables excluded from the SAM equation which have a significant impact on fertility. Regressions 2, 3, and 4 are useful for a systematic analysis of this question.

In equation 2, SAM is specified as a determinant of fertility along with age cohort impacts, family planning, and the death rate (which is highly negatively correlated with life expectancy).[50] Even though the results of equation 1 assure us that it is correlated with the death-rate, SAM seems to retain some independent explanatory power. Its estimated impact has the correct sign, is relatively large, and is a little less than twice the size of its estimated standard error.

When per capita income is specified as an additional variable in equation 3, the apparent relationship between SAM and fertility holds up quite well. Equation 4 tells quite a different story, however. With the inclusion of literacy (the second determinant of SAM in my first equation), the results suggest very strongly that the apparent independent impact of SAM was due to specification bias. The literacy coefficient itself has the correct sign, is relatively large, and significant by the classical criteria. The coefficient of SAM, on the other hand, drops to one-third of its former value and is less than one-half its estimated standard error.

For the reduced-form equation which is to be employed in the fertility change model, this is a hopeful result. The econometric estimates strongly suggest that there is no excluded determinant of SAM which adds significantly to the explanation of fertility once education and health effects are accounted for. I should add immediately that there is nothing final about this conclusion. As we shall see, the other cross-section results are not all upheld by the estimated fertility change equation. Literacy, which seems quite important in cross section, will become irrelevant when changes are considered. At the same time per capita income, seemingly irrelevant in cross section, will become significant in the change equation. As I argued in the previous chapter, the latter result may well be because percentage change in per capita income measures changing conditions for the poor with relatively small error variance.

(ii) Changes in fertility and family planning: A simultaneous model

We are now ready to consider the estimation of a reduced-form fertility change equation which can be used for prediction. As previously noted, its complement is a second equation which explains the change in family planning activity across countries during the same period. The left-hand variable in this complementary equation is the change in the Mauldin–Berelson index (which is the same as the level in the mid-1970s under the assumption that all national scores were effectively zero in 1960). The first right-hand variable is the change in the fertility rate. Another logical candidate would be some index of relevant institutional capacity. Among the available variables the secondary school enrolment ratio has been chosen as the most appropriate instrument since it simultaneously measures a society's training of potential cadres and the sophistication of the institutional resources available.

The problem of variable selection for the fertility change equation has been discussed in the preceding chapter. Given the available data, it seems appropriate to specify the change in the fertility rate as a function of percentage change in per capita income and change in female age cohort percentages, the infant mortality rate (for which we use the death-rate as a proxy), the literacy rate, and family planning activity.

In Figure 8, final estimates for the simultaneous two-equation model are presented.[51] As in the case of the output response model, the technique of three-stage least-squares has been employed in estimation. Prior experimentation has resulted in the adoption of some non-linear forms and the ultimate exclusion of variables whose parameters turned out to be insignificantly different from zero.

Among female age cohorts, only change in the group 25–34 had any apparent impact on the general fertility rate during the seventeen-year period, perhaps reflecting a world-wide rise in age at marriage. This result has been cross checked in several ways using alternative time change and cross-section specifications, and the basic conclusion seems to hold up. Therefore, the only age-specific component which shows up in the final estimate for the fertility rate equation is the change in the percentage representation of the age cohort 25–34.

FIGURE 8
Fertility Rate Change, 1960–1977—3SLS Results (*)

OBS

$$F\{t\} - F\{t-1\} = 187.338\star[W2534\{t\} - W2534\{t-1\}]$$
(98.439)   62

$$+ 9.6361\star[D\{t\} - D\{t-1\}] - .2470\star[D\{t\}\star\star 2 - D\{t-1\}\star\star 2]$$
  (2.8309)   (.0665)

$$- 15.4159\star[Q/P\{t\} - Q/P\{t-1\}]/[Q/P\{t-1\}]$$
  (5.868)

$$- 1.3122\star PLAN$$
  (.7308)

$$PLAN = .3245\star SEC - .1218\star[F\{t\} - F\{t-1\}]$$
         (.0764)   (.0295)   62

VARIABLES NOT PREVIOUSLY DEFINED

SEC = Secondary school enrolment ratio

(*) Standard errors in parentheses beneath coefficients.

For the two equations considered as a set, the results are quite strong. Changes in per capita income and the death-rate have an evident strong association with changes in fertility. In the case of the death-rate, it is particularly interesting that the parameter estimates are very close to those estimated in simple cross-section in section (i). The estimated coefficient moves rapidly toward unity (full compensation) as the death-rate declines. It should also be noted that the relatively superior performance of the constrained linear fertility model (see Appendix B) suggests that the crude death-rate is indeed a good proxy for the infant mortality rate. If the data had suggested a differential pattern of marginal impacts across cohorts, this would not have been the case.

In some ways, the result for the family planning index is the most interesting of the set. I do not think that this supply-side variable has previously been employed in published econometric work.[52] There are two aspects to the inclusion of family planning which are of particular note. The first, as expected, is that a pure demand-side equation is revealed as giving undue importance to the other variables. Preliminary experimentation (using ordinary least-squares) with a fertility change equation from which the Mauldin–Berelson index was excluded showed upward bias in the other estimates. The second aspect has to do with the effect of simultaneity. When the M-B index is introduced into a least-squares fertility equation like the ones in section (i), its coefficient is substantially larger and its degree of apparent statistical significance greater than in the simultaneous result. Again, this is exactly what econometric theory would have predicted. In any case, the final estimate is 'purged' of both sources of bias. The demand variables obviously remain important, and the estimated impact of change in family planning activity remains substantial.[53]

In the family planning equation, the change in the fertility rate is introduced as an endogenous variable. The estimated coefficient is strongly consistent with the hypothesis that a decline in the fertility rate has an impact on the propensity to undertake family planning programmes. (It is worth noting that the effect is statistically much stronger than the estimated simultaneous impact of planning on fertility decline.) The secondary school enrolment ratio is not a perfect proxy variable, but the strength of the result does suggest a significant role for institutional capacity.

As in the case of the output response model, certain plausible variables did not survive experimentation with the fertility model. Among the 'failed' variables, the biggest surprise was the literacy rate. As the results in section (i) indicate, the literacy rate generally does quite well in cross-section fertility regressions. Since literacy change contributes (as an endogenous variable) to output change, of course (see Chapter 3), the effect of schooling on fertility is still indirectly present.

(iii) Changes in the death-rate

In the full demographic model, prediction of the population growth rate requires a death-rate equation. For all other purposes (including the determination of fertility change), life expectancy would do as well. Thus, the guiding principle in experiments with the death-rate change equation was the theoretical necessity of near-parity with the life expectancy change equation discussed in Chapter 3. All the available measures of education and institutional capacity in health services were tried experimentally.

It was also necessary to consider age cohorts. As in the case of fertility rates, the death-rate is a weighted average of age-specific effects. Again, the problem of degrees of freedom has intervened to force the use of a relatively limited number of age groups in the econometric work. For the present purposes it was decided that division into three groups (0–14, 15–49, 50+) would be sufficient. Alternative

FIGURE 9
Crude Death-rate Changes, 1960-1977 (*)

$$D\{t\} - D\{t-1\} = 6.6523 - 1.06705 \star D\{t-1\} + .0193 \star D\{t-1\} \star \star 2$$
$$(1.6247) \quad (.1949) \quad\quad\quad (.0055)$$

OBS R★★2
64   .72

$$+ 2.4956E - 5 \star M\{t-1\} + 19.3986 \star [Y\{t\} - Y\{t-1\}]$$
$$(1.1442E - 5) \quad\quad (8.37428)$$

$$+ 19.8577 \star [O\{t\} - O\{t-1\}]$$
$$(7.5606)$$

VARIABLES NOT PREVIOUSLY DEFINED

Y = Children (1–15) as a percentage of the total population
O = Persons aged 50+ as a percentage of the total population

(*) Standard errors in parentheses beneath coefficients.
  Note that the 'autonomous' part of this equation could also be written:

$$D\{t\} = 6.6523 - .06705 \star D\{t-1\} + .0193 \star D\{t-1\} \star \star 2.$$

The autonomous component implies a smaller drop in the death-rate as the initial death-rate gets lower. The simplest way to see this is provided by the following calculated schedule relating initial death-rates to predicted autonomous declines:

$D\{t-1\}$	$D\{t\}$ (Predicted)	$[D\{t\} - D\{t-1\}]$ (Predicted)
25	17.04	−7.96
20	13.03	−6.97
15	9.99	−5.01
10	7.91	−2.09
8	7.36	−0.64

impact specificatons were evaluated, and again the constrained model with equal marginal cohort impacts was compatible with the data (see Appendix B).

It proved rather difficult to identify 'non-deterministic' factors which seem to have had a significant impact on death rate changes. Only the availability of medical personnel as indexed by doctors per capita, among all the plausible indices, has a significant multivariate association with death rate changes between 1960 and 1977. A model which also explicitly recognizes the presence of an autonomous component akin to 'technical progress', along with changes in the population percentages of children and older people, accounts for about 72 per cent of the variation in death rate changes in the sample for the period 1960-77. The final equation estimate is presented in Figure 9.

The age cohort coefficients can be interpreted to mean that the constant additive component in the death-rate attributable to these two vulnerable groups is about the same across the sample countries. As previously mentioned, the full set of results in the death-rate equation suggests that the marginal impact of medical personnel is not significantly different across cohorts.

PART III

SIMULATING SOCIO-ECONOMIC
DEVELOPMENT

CHAPTER 6

BUILDING A SIMULATION MODEL

In the first two parts of this book, a set of dynamic relations among output, population, and human resource variables has been specified and estimated econometrically. The results are useful in at least two ways. First, they cast some light on the validity of certain hypotheses concerning the links between human resource development and the growth of per capita income. Secondly, they provide a measure of the relative impact of right-hand side variables in the structural equations. Such a measure is appropriate for policy discussion, since it is clear that response sensitivities vary considerably.

Although individual parameter estimates provide the essential foundation for empirical analysis in cases such as this one, the complexity of the system being modelled precludes any reduction of the dynamic equations to a simple set of multipliers. Estimated coefficients do, however, provide measures of mean responsiveness which can be used for the simulation of dynamic behaviour. It is unrealistic to expect that the future evolution of poor LDCs will exactly reflect the evolution of their slightly better-endowed counterparts in the immediate past. To the extent that the fitted equations 'explain' observed behaviour under reasonable causal hypotheses, however, they provide a more accurate and consistent basis for projection than casual observation.

(i) Some uses and abuses of simulation

In policy research, a simulation model generally serves three main purposes: it forces the analyst to think comprehensively; it enforces consistency; and it facilitates detailed intellectual experiments with public policy instruments. In the initial phase of a project, it forces the researcher to consider carefully which features of a particular system seem to be understood and which require further study before the total behaviour of the system can be explained. It is an unfortunate tendency of the human imagination to leave difficult issues in the realm of the implicit whenever possible. When the growth process, for example, is studied in partial academic exercises, the researcher can focus on a few aspects and ignore the degree to which the results are sensible when viewed from the perspective of the whole system.

When a simulation model is being designed, this luxury is no longer available. The full set of relations among endogenous and predetermined variables must be worked out. If the model is to have much credibility, all of the hypothesized relations must be estimated econometrically under conditions in which the standard strictures dictated by statistical theory are respected.

Once the equations of a simulation model have been estimated and fitted together, the second major role of simulation comes into play. No matter how rigorous and comprehensive the intellect of the analyst, any first attempt to design equations which explain the operation of a particular system will suffer from conceptual errors. Most of these will be due to the fact that the mind is best suited for the consideration of problems in partial form. In considering the aggregate implication of an assembled set of partial views, the computer-driven simulation model is a singularly unforgiving associate. Inconsistent reasoning and incompatible specification of different relations in the model are quickly exposed, since simulation exercises yield absurd results. It is in the tracking down of these absurdities and subsequent reconsideration of partial relations from a systemic perspective that the utility of the simulation model as an intellectual tool becomes most apparent.

Finally, once both the preceding steps have been completed successfully, the simulation model can be employed for policy experiments. Since the computer does most of the work in this stage, it is in most respects the easiest and most enjoyable part of the process. At this point the full implications of the modelling exercise become clear. Generally, policy simulation models are designed under the assumption that public policy instruments are exogenous to the system being considered. This specification leaves the analyst free to examine the hypothetical evolution of the system under alternative assumptions concerning the time paths of the policy variables. At this stage, attention usually focuses on 'sensitivity analysis', in which one policy instrument is changed while the others are held constant.

Implicitly, sensitivity analysis is a form of cost-benefit analysis. Policy research is usually undertaken because public administrators are interested in effective approaches to the governance of systems in environments where several competing goals are valued and resources are limited. One important notion underlying the design and use of dynamic simulation models is that complex, interactive systems have behaviour patterns characterized by marked non-linearities and discontinuities. If this is the case, then all cost-equivalent policy packages are very unlikely to have the same consequences for the attainment of valued goals. It is easy to see that some approaches will be superior to others if they give relative weight to outcomes which have priority in the minds of administrators. What may be less immediately obvious is that in highly non-linear systems some cost-equivalent policy approaches can dominate others absolutely (that is, they can yield superior results along all of the valued dimensions).

It is this latter possibility which is undoubtedly the source of the evident allure of simulation models. Unfortunately, too much can be made of this. It is all too easy for public administrators to throw up their hands in the face of daily pressures and leave the design and interpretation of models of the complex systems which they must confront to the 'experts'. This 'black box' syndrome has become quite common, and it can be the only possible explanation for the wide-spread acclamation and acceptance given to the conclusions of models so evidently flawed as the Urban Dynamics and World Dynamics systems used by the Systems Dynamics Group at MIT to justify sweeping conclusions concerning problems as diverse as urban renewal and the philosophy of limited growth for the world as a whole.[54]

In fact, simulation models can only be valuable to the extent that they are not 'black boxes'. 'Counter-intuitive' results are useful results only if they can be shown to be intuitive once the structure of the system is clearly seen. In order for this to be possible, over-complexity in the design of model equation systems is best avoided. The true value of simulation exercises lies in their ability to test the internal consistency of a set of ideas about a particular process. If seemingly-plausible sets of estimated relations yield peculiar results when they are fitted together into a model, then two conclusions are possible: first, the thinking of the researcher may suffer from some important inconsistency which must be corrected. Secondly, it may be that the peculiar results are themselves reasonable when the behaviour of the entire system is considered.

In either case, it is obvious that no conclusions can be drawn from simulation exercises if the equations on which they are based are too complex to be sorted out retrospectively. In a good simulation model, the source of any peculiar result can be traced down and analysed. At this level, the model becomes tremendously valuable as an aid to learning because it uses the speed of the computer to augment the analytical capabilities of the policy analyst. However, this argument ought to help persuade the reader that any simulation experiment should be considered carefully in the context of model design and the potential role of factors which have been excluded from the model altogether.

(ii) Assembling the equations

Having alerted the reader in a general way to the pitfalls in this process, I will begin my discussion of the model with an examination of its essential components and the role which they play in the whole system. The most fundamental distinction to be drawn is between the elements which are ultimately endogenous and those which are exogenous. Endogenous variables are those whose future values will in the final analysis be determined by the interaction of model equations. Exogenous variables, on the other hand, are those whose complete future time paths must be specified as a prerequisite for running the model at all.

While this distinction between variable types is certainly the most important one in the modelling exercise, there is another which is also quite significant. Not all variables which are 'ultimately endogenous' in the sense defined above have been treated as endogenous in the econometric estimations reported in Chapters 3 and 5. Recall that in many of the fitted equations, initial values of certain variables join lagged changes as predetermined variables in the identification of system coefficients. The use of the two-block structure (accumulation-response) reflects a recursive view of the growth process which has already been explained.

Thus, many of the variables which are predetermined in the econometric estimates will themselves change intertemporally as a simulation exercise joins the two equation blocks in dynamic interaction. With the distinction among 'endogenous', 'exogenous', and 'predetermined' now firmly in mind, we can proceed to a discussion of the roles played by particular model variables in the simulation process.

The separation of model variables into categories corresponding to the terms used above depends upon a fundamental view of the world which has been built into the equation system. Basically, this view can be summarized as follows: it may be reasonable to regard public policy instruments as independent levers for influencing the future of a particular system. However, it is unreasonable to suppose that those instruments can be applied in any kind of a vacuum. History matters in the sense that the conditions prevailing in a society at any particular time will have important consequences for the future evolutionary possibilities of the system. A model which aspires to serious consideration must build in these initial conditions in a plausible way.

For convenience of exposition, all of the predetermined variables in the present model are presented along with the endogenous variables in Figure 10.

A glance at Figure 10 makes it obvious that our estimation exercise has produced a model whose data requirements are substantial. When the equations are fitted together, the resulting system requires initial values for a large number of variables as well as hypothesized future time paths for the policy variables. Although the list of variables is

FIGURE 10
Simulation Model Variables

PREDETERMINED VARIABLES

Policy variables	*Initial conditions*
Medical Personnel	Birth-rate
Schooling	Death-rate
	Population
	Adult population
	Investment rate
	Nutrition level
	Life expectancy
	Literacy
	Per capita income

ENDOGENOUS VARIABLES

Accumulation	*Response*
Population change	Output change
Capital stock change	Nutrition change
Age cohort change	Literacy change
Labour force change	Life expectancy change
	Family planning

useful in separating them into intellectual categories, the precise way in which they will fit into the simulation model still warrants discussion.

A look back at the estimated equations will aid considerably here in determining the role played by different variables in the system. Perhaps the most useful way in which to discuss alternative roles is to identify the data which must be specified before a simulation model based on the estimated equations can even be run. Obviously, all of the truly exogenous variables such as policy instruments must be known. As for the rest, the best vehicle for organization may again be sequential consideration of blocks and equations. The relevant econometric estimates are summarized in Figure 11.

In the response block, output growth determination depends on prior knowledge of the labour force growth rate and the growth of the capital stock. Evaluation of the nutrition equation depends upon prior knowledge of the initial level of nutrition, along with the growth rate of population. In the literacy equation, additional information requirements are imposed by the need for data on primary school enrolment ratios during the relevant period for the most recent adult age cohort. The growth rate of the adult population is also required for the evaluation of this equation. Finally, the life expectancy change

FIGURE 11
The Estimated Equations

RESPONSE

(1) Output
$$\langle dq \rangle = .012 + .146 \star \langle dk \rangle + .565 \star \langle dl \rangle + 1.011 \star \langle dn \rangle + .0096 \star [E\{T\} - E\{t-1\}]$$

(2) Nutrition
$$\langle dn \rangle = -.040 + [3.259 - .674 \ln N] \star [\langle dq \rangle - \langle dp \rangle] + .042 \star \ln [(Q/P)/N]$$

(3) Literacy
$$E\{t\} - E\{t-1\} \star [1/(1 + \langle da \rangle)] = -.996 + .755 \star S \star [\langle da \rangle/(1 + \langle da \rangle)]$$
$$+ 12.291 \star [\langle dq \rangle - \langle dq \rangle]$$

(4) Life expectancy
$$\langle dh \rangle = -.124 + 6.948 \star (1/H) + [.573 - .144 \ln H] \star [\langle dq \rangle - \langle dp \rangle]$$
$$+ .142 \star \langle dh\{t-1\} \rangle + .077 \star \langle dn\{t-1\} \rangle + .027 \star [E/H]$$
$$- 1.10E - 5 \star [M/H] + .010 \star [S/H]$$

ACCUMULATION

(5) Investment
$$I\{t\} - I\{t-1\} = 8.3445 - .6939 \star I\{t-1\}$$
$$+ 5.3017 \star [Q/P\{t\} - Q/P\{t-1\}]/[Q/P\{t-1\}]$$
$$+ 3.0705 \star [E\{t\} - E\{t-1\}]/I\{t-1\}$$
$$+ 2.1829 \star [H\{t\} - H\{t-1\}]/I\{t-1\}$$

(6) Fertility rate
$$F\{t\} - F\{t-1\} = 187.388 \star [W2534\{t\} - W2534\{t-1\}]$$
$$+ 9.6361 \star [D\{t\} - D\{t-1\}] - .2470 \star [D\{t\} \star\star 2 - D\{t-1\} \star\star 2]$$
$$- 15.4159 \star [Q/P\{t\} - Q/P\{t-1\}]/[Q/P\{t-1\}]$$
$$- 1.3122 \star PLAN$$

(7) Family planning
$$PLAN = .3245 \star SEC - .1218 \star [F\{t\} - F\{t-1\}]$$

(8) Death-rate
$$D\{t\} - D\{t-1\} = 6.6523 - 1.06705 \star D\{t-1\} + .0193 \star D\{t-1\} \star\star 2$$
$$+ 2.4956E - 5 \star M\{t-1\} + 19.3986 \star [Y\{t\} - Y\{t-1\}]$$
$$+ 19.8577 \star [O\{t\} - O\{t-1\}]$$

equation depends upon the initial level of life expectancy, change in life expectancy during the preceding period, change in nutrition during the preceding period, and the initial levels of literacy, schooling, and medical personnel availability. If all these data are known, then the response equations will generate contemporaneous changes in output, nutrition, and literacy. In addition, life expectancy change can be calculated.

It is obvious that some of the prerequisite data for the response block are immediate products of the accumulation block. In this block, for example, the determination of the investment rate leads immediately to the capital stock change variable (capital stock change/ initial output) which is used in the output change equation. This new investment rate, in turn, depends upon the investment rate in the preceding period and recent changes in per capita income, literacy, and life expectancy.

The accumulation block is also the locus for the calculation of the population growth rate, which is the difference between the crude birth-rate and the crude death-rate. The crude birth-rate can be calculated once we know the appropriate female age cohort percentage and recent changes in the death-rate, per capita income, and family planning activities. Calculation of the death-rate in turn depends upon the prior death-rate, age cohort changes, and the availability of medical personnel.

(iii) The model

With all this as prelude, it is now time to turn to the simulation equations themselves. The preceding discussion will, we hope, have cleared the methodological thickets sufficiently to allow for a relatively clear view of the process being described. The 'Closed Economy' model has been used as the foundation for the response block here.

The simulation model has been built around the eight estimated equations which are presented in Figure 11. Many non-stochastic equations have been introduced for appropriate variable definitions, the tracking of age cohort groups, and other 'housekeeping' functions. In addition, three regression results have been necessary for the replication of typical performance in schooling, medical care, and institutional capacity for family planning over simulation runs. The model is presented in Figure 12. Equations 1 and 2 have been generated by fitting asymptotic regression equations to cross country data for 1977. For the prediction of typical progress in secondary schooling (the exogenous variable in the family planning equation), a log-linear regression has been fitted to 1977 cross country data. The result is simulation equation 3.

In Figure 12, the symbols are those which have been employed in the estimation sections, so that redefinition does not seem to be necessary. Wherever possible, the estimation results reported in Chapters 3 and 5 have been transferred exactly into the simulation. Some adjustments have been necessary for the completion of the model, however. Most of these are designed to compensate for the fact that the period

FIGURE 12
Simulation Model

(1) $S = 102.53 - 3030.69/(Q/P)$

(2) $M = -346.02 + 1885320/(Q/P)$

(3) $SEC = \exp(-2.4124)\star(Q/P)\star\star.9348$

(4) $PM1 = 1 - D(-1)/1000$

(5) $PM2 = (1 - D(-1)/1000)\star\star7$

(6) $P17 = P(-1) \star B(-1)/1000\star(1 + PM1 + PM1\star\star2 + PM1\star\star3 + PM1\star\star4$
      $+ PM1\star\star5 + PM1\star\star6)$

(7) $P814 = P17(-1)\star PM2$

(8) $Y = P17 + P814$

(9) $A = (A(-1) + P814(-1))\star PM2$

(10) $P = Y + A$

(11) $PY = Y/P$

(12) $W1519 = 5/7\star.5\star P814(-1)\star PM2$

(13) $W2024 = W1519(-1)\star PM2$

(14) $W2529 = W2024(-1)\star PM2$

(15) $W3034 = W2529(-1)\star PM2$

(16) $W3539 = W3034(-1)\star PM2$

(17) $W4044 = W3539(-1)\star PM2$

(18) $W4549 = W4044(-1)\star PM2$

(19) $W2534 = W2529 + W3034$

(20) $W1549 = W1519 + W2024 + W2529 + W3034 + W3539 + W4044$
      $+ W4549$

(21) $PW2534 = W2534/W1549$

(22) $PO = 1 - PY - 2\star W1549/P$

(23) $DP = (P - P(-1))/P(-1)$

(24) $DA = (A - A(-1))/A(-1)$

(25) $DL = DA$

(26) $DK = 7\star I(-1)/100$

(27) $DQ = .012 + .146\star DK + .565\star DL + 1.011\star DN + .0096\star(E - E(-1))$

(28) $DN = -.04 + (3.259 - .674\star LOG(N(-1)))\star(DQ - DP)$
      $+ .042\star LOG((Q/P)\,(-1)/N(-1))$

(29) $E = E(-1)\star(1/(1 + DA)) - .996 + .755\star(S(-1) + S(-2))/2\star(DA/(1 + DA))$
      $+ 12.291\star(DQ - DP)$

Figure 12 (*cont*)

(30) $DH = -.124 + 6.948 \star 1/H(-1) + .142 \star DH(-1)$
$+ (.573 - .144 \star LOG(H(-1))) \star (DQ - DP) + .077 \star DN(-1)$
$+ .027 \star E(-1)/H(-1) + 1.10E - 5 \star M(-1)/H(-1) + .01 \star S(-1)/H(-1)$

(31) $Q/P = Q/P(-1) \star (1 + DQ - DP)$

(32) $H = H(-1) \star (1 + DH)$

(33) $I = 8.34446 + .30611 \star I(-2) + 5.30167 \star ((Q/P)$
$- (Q/P)(-2))/(Q/P)(-2) + 3.07052 \star (E - E(-2))/I(-2)$
$+ 2.18293 \star (H - H(-2))/I(-2)$

(34) $N = N(-1) \star (1 + DN)$

(35) $D = 6.6523 - .0671 \star D(-2) + .0193 \star D(-2) \star\star 2 + 2.4956E - 5 \star M(-2)$
$+ 19.3986 \star (PY - PY(-2)) + 19.8577 \star (PO - PO(-2))$

(36) $BC = .15902 \star SEC(-1) - 27.1634 \star (PW2534 - PW2534(-1))$
$- 1.3972 \star (D - D(-1)) + .03582 \star (D \star\star 2 - D(-1) \star\star 2)$
$+ 2.23525 \star ((Q/P) - (Q/P)(-1))/(Q/P)(-1)$

(37) $PLAN = IF\ BC + PPLAN\ (-1)\ LT\ 30\ THEN\ BC\ ELSE\ 30 - PPLAN\ (-1)$

(38) $PPLAN = PPLAN\ (-1) + PLAN$

(39) $DFR = 187.338 \star (PW2534 - PW2534(-1)) + 9.63614 \star (D - D(-1))$
$- .2470 \star (D \star\star 2 - D(-1) \star\star 2)$
$- 15.4159 \star [Q/P - Q/P(-1)]/Q/P(-1) - 1.3122 \star PLAN$

(40) $FR = IF\ FR(-1) + DFR\ GE\ 40\ THEN\ FR(-1)\ ELSE\ 40$

(41) $PF = W1549/P$

(42) $B = FR \star PF$

used for modelling here is seven years. Thus, the projected capital growth variable is produced by multiplying the anticipated yearly investment rate by seven (recall that the capital growth measure in the fitted output equation is defined as (capital change)/(initial output), so that the simulation equation is tailored to the econometric approach). Besides the adjustment for seven-year periods and some necessary divisions by 100 or 1000 to produce appropriately scaled rates, the equations are either definitions, year-to-year adjustments of initial conditions, or directly transcribed econometric results.

CHAPTER 7

AN ILLUSTRATION: HUMAN RESOURCE
POLICY AND CHANGES IN THE
QUALITY OF LIFE

Such a model-building effort can be justified if the result holds some promise of providing information which could not be gained by inspection of individual econometric results. In this case, there are simply too many such results for their total implication to be grasped through separate consideration. Rather than calculating a set of fixed multipliers, we are forced to conduct policy experiments with the knowledge that outcomes will be sensitive to initial conditions as well as continuing levels of public activity. Since the notion that 'history matters' seems eminently sensible in any case, this indeterminacy should probably be regarded as a strength of the simulation approach.

(i) Representative data

Obviously, believable policy experiments must be founded on believable initial conditions in this case. Although it is certainly possible to construct a 'typical' LDC from central tendencies in distributions of socio-economic data, it seems advisable to allow for major regional differences by experimenting with typical poor-country data for different regions. For the present purposes, three sets of initial conditions have therefore been constructed. The numbers are broadly representative of the recent historical experiences of poor countries in Africa, Southern America, and South Asia.

Some of the historical indices presented in Figure 13 are quite different, while others (such as initial birth-rates) are similar. It might have been desirable to incorporate more variance into initial conditions for the sake of comparison, but the interest here has been focused on an attempt to use numbers which are representative. With these numbers (and a large additional set of observations on other variables such as the GDP growth rate) as initial conditions, the full 42-equation simulation model has been run through a sequence of seven-year periods to the year 2026. The resulting baseline simulation has been used for comparison with the results of some policy experiments.

FIGURE 13
Initial Conditions

	AFRICA	SOUTH AMERICA	SOUTH ASIA
Per Capita Income			
1960	50	210	60
1970	57.5	268.8	91.4
1977	63.8	330.4	96
Literacy Rate			
1960	10	39	15
1970	15	50	20
1977	20	63	21
Life Expectancy			
1960	37	43	44
1970	40	48	48
1977	42	52	51
Calorie Sufficiency			
1960	85	69	84
1970	78	76	94
1977	78	77	93
Birth-rate			
1960	49	48	49
1970	48	47	47
1977	44.5	40	44
Death-rate			
1960	27	23	23
1970	24	19	18
1977	20.2	16.6	16.5
Investment Rate			
1960	13	12.4	12.5
1970	14	18.8	19
1977	17.7	22.8	18
Primary School Enrolment Ratio			
1960	10	64	52
1970	40	80	69
1977	55	93	71
Population per Doctor			
1960	37706	8978	31076
1970	32788	7014	20718
1977	29220	5361	19299

(ii) Equilibrium traps revisited

Before the illustrative simulation runs are discussed, it is worth harking back for a moment to the discussion of genealogy in Chapter 1. As I noted there, this work represents a branch in the family tree of economic-demographic modelling which extends back through the work of Hazledine–Moreland (1977), Enke (1963), and Nelson (1956). These prior works are theoretical or empirical investigations of 'equilibrium traps' which may stymie development attempts. The Nelson trap can occur if the death rate declines faster than the savings rate rises as per capita income increases. If economies get stuck in this 'low-level' trap, they are condemned to fall back to subsistence in the absence of some outside intervention.

The Enke 'high-level' equilibrium trap is unavoidable without technical progress. In the face of fixed national resource endowments, a developing society will experience rising tension between population growth and diminishing returns to investment until it reaches the growth limit on its 'zero improvement curve'. Hazledine and Moreland have estimated a set of economic-demographic equations for three poor regions (Africa, Asia, Latin America) and have used them for simulation runs which seem to confirm the Enke version.

What is left to add to this tradition? A great deal, as all of these scholars themselves have noted. My own contribution to this literature is intended to be threefold. First, I have used a relatively large data set to estimate all my equations in dynamic form. Secondly, I have explicitly incorporated age cohorts into my model, so that important changes in the labour force and the population of women of reproductive age can be tracked through time. Finally, I have explicitly introduced 'sources of growth' which are ignored by all the prior work.

Education is the most familiar of these, and it is instructive to consider the likely effect of excluding it from a growth model. As I noted in Chapter 1, the role played by schooling in Western economic growth is generally acknowledged. Improvement in schooling has been an integral part of the recent historical experience of almost all societies, in fact. To relegate education to the realm of the exogenous in a growth model (as Nelson, Enke, and Hazledine–Moreland all do) seems questionable. It also eliminates from the model an important source of technical progress which may allow it to move smoothly past the low-level equilibrium trap.

In my model, education is joined by health, nutrition, and family planning capacity in the full set of human resource variables. It is plausible to suppose that the dynamic impact of typical improvements in these variables would be sufficient to propel the economy steadily forward. My first set of simulation runs evaluates this hypothesis by contrasting the results for LOW, MEDIUM, and HIGH commitments to education and family planning. Africa and South Asia are employed as cases.

The MEDIUM simulation reflects the 'normal' case which has been built into the model. Family planning is determined endogenously in this case. In each period, the primary school enrolment ratio is predicted using the results of a simple asymptotic regression fitted to cross-country data for the year 1977. In the HIGH simulation, the same model is employed, but the literacy rate is given an exogenous boost of 30 per cent for the period 1977–84. The LOW results reflect the predicted evolution of the hypothetical African and South Asian societies under the assumption that the primary school enrolment ratio is frozen at 0.20 and no family planning activity is undertaken. The schooling assumption is quite pessimistic, of course. Both societies have primary enrolment considerably above 0.20 at the present time. I have included the LOW case in deference to the ancestors, since it most closely replicates their total exclusion of human resource considerations.

So that the impacts of these alternative assumptions may be clearly demonstrated, the three education simulations have been run through twelve simulation periods (or eighty-four hypothetical years). It would obviously be wrong to attach much significance to the precise numbers produced by such long runs. Their advantage lies in the pattern of non-linear response which they clearly illustrate and their implications for the 'equilibrium trap' approach. Figure 14 reproduces the simulation paths for four measures of the quality of life (income, life expectancy, literacy, nutrition) and the birth-rate.

The time plots of outcomes in Figure 14 reveal some of the implications of such drastically differing approaches to education. In the LOW case, the pervasive impression of relative stagnation does not conflict seriously with the notion of a low-level equilibrium trap. Literacy stagnates or declines, and nutrition deteriorates for at least fifty years in both cases. Life expectancy increase is strongly constrained. The birth-rate falls a little, but population growth continues scarcely abated as the death-rate continues to be propelled downward. The autonomous component of investment assures some mild increase in per capita income, but even this increment would probably have been eliminated if no schooling at all had been imposed on the model.

Besides the inclusion of some schooling, there is one apparent reason why my model does not fully replicate the Hazledine–Moreland results in the LOW case. My demographic equations are estimated in changes rather than levels, and incorporate much more recent information

FIGURE 14a
Simulation Results—Africa

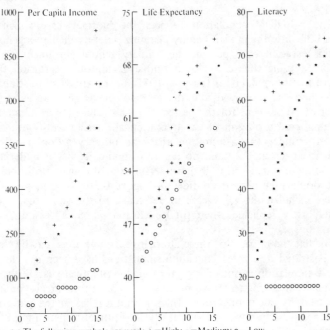

(∗) The following symbols are used: +=High; ∗=Medium; o =Low

than that employed in the prior study. My results are quite different from, and relatively more optimistic than, theirs.[55] The optimism is reinforced by the MEDIUM simulation runs, which I consider the most realistic. On the whole, everything goes right in these results. If the poor African and South Asian societies follow the human resource path which has already been blazed in Latin America and East/South-east Asia, the predicted future is promising. By the eightieth year of the simulation, for example, the African society has moved from a per capita income of 64 dollars to about 700 dollars. The literacy rate has moved from 20 per cent to 70 per cent; life expectancy from 42 years to 68 years; and per capita calorie sufficiency from 78 per cent of the norm proposed by the UN Food and Agricultural Organization (FAO) to 120 per cent. Starting from a slightly higher base, the South Asian society does just as well.

In the HIGH case, the result of a one-period boost in education

FIGURE 14b
Simulation Results—South Asia

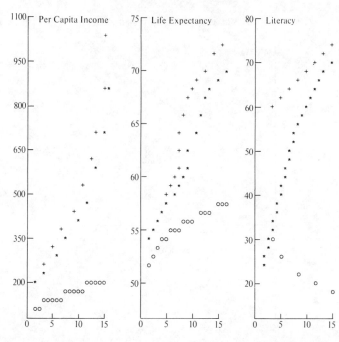

is even more striking. The model equations predict that this shift will generate a time path which diverges substantially from that of the MEDIUM case for most of the crucial model variables. An interesting variation on this theme is provided by the growth of literacy, where inherently asymptotic behaviour produces an apparent convergence for time paths in the MEDIUM and HIGH cases.

Is all this simply cockeyed optimism? Obviously, I cannot answer this question, but I take comfort in the fact that no one else can either. Pessimism has become so fashionable during the past decade that an attractive future for LDCs under reasonable assumptions seems automatically suspect. It is worth reiterating that my simulated version of the future is based entirely on an econometric analysis of economic and demographic dynamics in the immediate past. I suppose that I could be accused of deliberately structuring my model to yield optimistic conclusions from the start, and it would certainly be pleasing to claim such profound insight. Having wrestled with many separate econometric problems, the complications associated with large data

FIGURE 14c

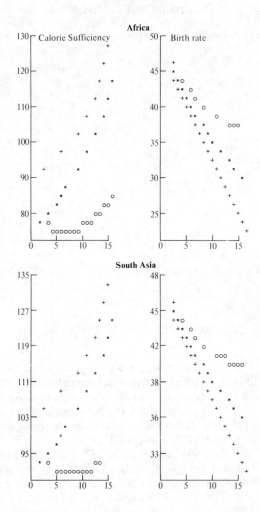

sets, and the need for many demographic house-keeping equations in the simulation model, I confess to total inability to foresee the outcome before I set the computer in motion. In retrospect, of course, the relative balance of forces revealed by the equations has become 'obvious' to me.

There is certainly nothing counter-intuitive about the basic structure of the model itself. It is therefore not difficult to trace the general reasons for the behaviour predicted in the LOW, MEDIUM, and HIGH cases. An increase in literacy, for example, has three mutually reinforcing effects. There are immediate responses predicted for the output growth rate and the investment rate. These reinforce one another in producing income gains, which in turn join with other variables in inducing gains in nutrition, health, and education. At the same time, the induced rise in the per capita income level produces a response in death-rates and fertility rates. Although the effect of the death-rate decline is perverse in the sense that the sluggish responsiveness of fertility to infant mortality changes yields a positive impact on population growth, the direct impact of income change on the fertility rate is a compensating factor. The net effect of all these forces is a simultaneous steepening in the growth rate of output and a flattening in the growth rate of population. The advantage produced by the initial surge tends to persist through time, as indicated by the comparison with the MEDIUM case.

The relative stagnation apparent in the LOW case can be explained with reference to many of the phenomena mentioned above. With primary schooling frozen at a very low level, successive age cohorts arrive at adulthood with very low literacy rates. At the same time, no impetus is provided for family planning activity as an additional instrument for lowering the fertility rate. The cumulative impact of these two weaknesses is seen in a birth-rate which is so persistently high as to overwhelm the prevailing death-rate. In addition, the absence of the self-reinforcing dynamic interaction between output and education growth leaves the economy dependent on the increment provided by changes in the capital stock and the physical quantity of labour, rather than the quality of labour.

The final result of this relative stagnation in per capita income and human resource indices is a country whose population is much larger and much poorer (in per capita terms) than that predicted by the MEDIUM and HIGH cases. The exponential nature of the accumulation parameters produces a long-run aggregate GDP which is larger for the MEDIUM and HIGH cases.

The contrasting simulations reported here are not intended to provide a full illustration of the behavioural dynamics of the model, nor do they provide more than a very partial view of the kinds of behaviour predicted by the model under alternative assumptions about initial conditions and public policies. They do suggest that the model as specified and estimated accords a very powerful role to both education and family planning activities in the determination of long-run social and economic outcomes.

(iii) Benefits and costs in human resource programmes

From the perspective of public policy analysis, it is of course insufficient to use an apparently powerful impact to justify increased investment in schooling or family planning activities. A consideration of the significance of simulation outcomes must depend on some consideration of relative marginal net benefits, whenever this is possible. A logical alternative to the use of public funds for the promotion of human resources would be their diversion to physical investment. Since an augmented investment rate would increase the growth rate of output, with subsequent impacts on income, human resources, and fertility, it might well be argued that the best approach to the human resource problem is an augmented growth rate of the capital stock.[56]

It is apparent that this kind of debate can be resolved only through a modelling approach which is at least akin to that taken here. Because initial conditions clearly count, the way in which resource-equivalent policy interventions occur should have consequences for final outcomes. At the same time, a consideration of marginal net benefits must take dynamic relations explicitly into account. A policy which moves resources directly into physical investment will have an immediate impact on per capita income and visible short-run impacts on other socio-economic variables as the effect of enhanced family income spreads through the system.

Investments in human resources, by contrast, will have general impacts which become apparent over longer periods of time. An increase in the number of primary enrolments in the 1980s will begin to have a visible impact on socio-economic outcomes during the succeeding decade, as more literate adults join the labour force and make decisions about optimal family size. An intensification of family planning activity might well take even longer to demonstrate its full effect, since the impact of a permanently lowered fertility rate on the evolution of per capita income would only become apparent after a succession of smaller groups for each age cohort had passed into the system.[57]

For all the reasons just cited, it is difficult to consider policy experiments in this context without the introduction of much disagreeable complexity. Different policies will generate different time paths, not just for per capita incomes but for other variables which are important in determining the physical quality of life (PQLI). Some investments have longer gestation periods than others as well, and again this fact applies to the evolution of PQLI variables as well as per capita income. Thus, trade-off experiments of the type proposed here cannot yield unambiguous conclusions unless the results of one policy dominate the results of others absolutely and at every future point in time.

The final and most aggravating complexity stems from the necessity for cost estimates. Unless the policy experiments are based on inputs which reflect roughly equivalent costs, all comparisons are meaningless. Let us begin with an attempt to confront the costing problem.

(iv) Equivalent physical and human resource expenditures

The methodology underlying my equivalent cost estimates is not at all elaborate. All my basic data have been borrowed from a World Bank study by Burki and Voorhoeve (1977). The criterion for judgement has been 'essential equivalence', given the approximate, aggregative nature of the data. Once the methodology has been presented, the numbers for specific regional cases will be presented in tabular form in Figure 15.

The 'foil' for comparison in these experiments is the 50-year behaviour of the baseline model for each regional case, under the assumption that the investment rate is raised by one per cent only for the seven-year period from 1977 to 1984. The calculation of this increment is perfectly straightforward. Given the measured national income and investment rate in any particular year, the value of a one per cent increment in the investment rate can be obtained by simple multiplication.

While per capita income levels in this study have been measured in 1960 US dollars, the World Bank cost estimates are denominated in 1975 US dollars. Since the US price index went up by something more than 100 per cent between 1960 and 1975, all cost estimates have simply been halved to reflect 1960 equivalents. Given the index number problems which plague this sort of calculation and a common preference for currency overvaluation, this deflator may be quite conservative. Once the cost corrections have been made, the generation of equivalent activity numbers is quite simple. Since the assumptions underlying comparisons for schooling and family planning are quite different, it undoubtedly makes sense to discuss them separately.

In the case of schooling, the World Bank data are divided (by region) into four cost categories—teachers' salaries, materials, administrative overheads, and capital costs. The appropriate unit for cost measurement is a little difficult to define in this context, but the Bank estimates are standardized per student-place. Since shift systems are quite common in schools, there can obviously be more students than student-places in the system at any one time. Teachers' salaries are calculated per 50 student-places; materials costs are simply set at 7 per cent of salaries, and overheads are calculated as an additional 3 per cent of salaries. Separate figures for capital costs per student-place have been included in the Bank estimates.

The need for rough comparability between the investment experiment and the re-allocation to schooling introduces a problem in the appropriate treatment of capital cost in this context. Since the seven-year boost should be regarded as a one-time increase for the sake of equivalence, it does not seem appropriate to allocate all capital cost per new student to the expansion. For simplicity, the following compromise has been adopted: only recurrent costs have been employed in the schooling calculations, but student-places have been adopted as the basic unit for cost estimation. The use of a conservative deflator along with student-places should approximately balance the suppression of capital costs from the calculation, since recurrent costs are heavily dominant in the determination of total education costs and capital costs would have to be spread over several student generations in a full intertemporal calculation.

In the case of family planning, the determination of 'essential equivalence' has been even rougher. Although use has been made of the Mauldin–Berelson index of family planning activity in the econometric work, no apparent basis exists for converting M–B scores into cost estimates. For the present purposes, therefore, the opposite tack has been taken. Under the assumption that family planning teams in rural areas would be in many ways comparable to community health workers, the World Bank cost estimates for health teams were used for the conversion of investment values to team-equivalents. These team-equivalents were then compared with the female population in reproductive cohorts to determine the capacity for coverage provided by such an expenditure. In no case was the ratio higher than 200 females per three-person team—seemingly quite a modest ratio.

With these relatively low ratios in hand, I proceeded to the second part of the family planning exercise. Some experimentation with the simulation model by region was used to determine the minimum value of an exogenous boost to the M–B index which would generate a final (fifty-year) per capita income growth higher than that achieved by the investment increment. In most cases, the requisite boost was only 2 (out of a total possible M–B score of 30); in one case, it was 3. My own conclusion is that family planning investment at the margin is at least equivalent to physical investment if long run outcomes are most highly valued. In fact, the awarding of an M–B score of only 2 to such a drastic expansion of family planning personnel seems quite conservative.

Since the family planning experiment involved the prior calculation of nearly-equivalent income outcomes, it may seem unnecessary to include any simulation runs which can be compared with those for schooling and investment. The family planning simulations do seem to be of interest, however, for two reasons: first, they reveal the extent to which 'essential equivalence' in income outcomes is matched by relative performance for the other PQLI variables. Secondly, they facilitate a clearer perception of the different pattern of relative outcomes at different points in time.

All relevant calculations are presented in Figure 15. In the Schooling set, per capita income and population are combined to yield total national income. One per cent of this figure is taken as the hypothetical investment increment. Total recurrent cost per student-place is then calculated using the indicated estimates for teachers' salaries and mark-ups for materials and overheads. Division of the increment by the unit recurrent cost yields the number of new students supported by the additional revenue (under the heroic assumption, of course, that no constraint exists in teaching capacity). Finally, the new students can be combined with total children in the primary-school age population to produce the one-period boost in the primary enrolment ratio. In the South American case, the resulting estimate is much greater than 1.00. Numbers larger than one are quite common in LDCs, because older uneducated children are attracted to primary schools as capacity expands.

The basis for the family planning numbers in Figure 15 should be relatively clear. The indicated investment increment has simply been divided by the cost per three-person team to yield the number of team-equivalents. This result is in turn divided into the number of females of reproductive age to produce a ratio of females to teams.

(v) Outcomes: Africa and Latin America

We are now ready to consider the implications of alternative investment strategies whose costs are (very!) roughly equivalent. All results should be judged in the context of the many simplifying assumptions which have been made. With this fundamental point in mind, the trade-off simulation results presented in Figure 16 are specified as relative rankings at the end of each seven-year simulation period. It is clear that relative rankings can change through time, and that slow starters do not necessarily lose the race. In such long-run processes, of course, entire lives can be lived as the race proceeds and the question of an appropriate discount rate must intrude. If, as some have argued, the long-run social discount rate for an entire society should be zero in such cases, then endurance should always be given precedence over speed in the judgement of final outcomes.

The African and South American cases have been selected for this illustration because their initial conditions are in most respects quite

FIGURE 15
Comparative Cost Estimates—Simulation Experiments

(1) RECURRENT EDUCATION COST ESTIMATES

Region	Salary	Materials	Overhead
Africa	1146/50	.07 × salary	.03 × salary
S. America	1334/50	.07 × salary	.03 × salary
S. Asia	899/50	.07 × salary	.03 × salary

CALCULATION OF EQUIVALENT SCHOOLING EFFORT

	Income/Capita	Population (mill.)	Increment (mill.)
Africa	63.77	6.866	4.379
S. America	330.36	5.734	18.944
S. Asia	95.97	69.376	66.580

	Primary-Age Population (mill.)	Primary School Enrolment Ratio	New Students (mill.)	Increment to Primary Enrolment Ratio
Africa	1.474	55.00	.175	11.85
S. America	1.112	93.36	.649	58.41
S. Asia	14.074	70.95	3.387	24.05

(2) FAMILY PLANNING CALCULATIONS

	Increment	Cost/Team	No. of Teams
Africa	4.379	599.5	7,304
S. America	18.944	599.5	31,600
S. Asia	66.580	599.5	111,059

	Reproductive-Age Women/Team	M–B Score for Equivalency
Africa	193	3
S. America	39	2
S. Asia	127	2

different. An intertemporal time path of relative ranking is provided for per capita income, literacy, life expectancy, and nutrition. For each case, the same basic experiment has been run. In the interests of clarity, I will summarize the generation of cost equivalent inputs. In the Investment simulation, the investment rate has been autonomously increased by 1 per cent of GDP for one seven-year simulation period. For School, equivalent resources are devoted to increasing the primary school enrolment ratio during the same seven-year period, using World Bank estimates of recurrent cost for personnel, materials, and overheads by world region.

FIGURE 16
Trade-off Results—Africa

	Investment	School	Planning
Income			
1984	1	2	2
1991	1	2	3
1998	2	1	3
2005	2	1	3
2012	3	1	2
2019	3	2	1
2026	2	3	1
Literacy			
1984	1	2	2
1991	2	1	3
1998	2	1	3
2005	2	1	3
2012	2	1	3
2019	2	1	3
2026	2	1	3
Life Expectancy			
1984	1	2	3
1991	1	2	3
1998	2	1	3
2005	2	1	3
2012	2	1	3
2019	2	1	3
2026	2	1	3
Nutrition			
1984	1	2	2
1991	1	2	3
1998	3	1	2
2005	3	1	2
2012	3	1	2
2019	3	2	1
2026	3	2	1

Trade-off Results—South America

	Investment	School	Planning
Income			
1984	1	2	2
1991	2	1	3
1998	2	1	3
2005	2	1	3
2012	2	1	3
2019	2	1	3
2026	3	1	2

Figure 16 (cont)

Literacy	Investment	School	Planning
1984	1	2	2
1991	2	1	3
1998	2	1	3
2005	2	1	3
2012	3	1	2
2019	3	1	2
2026	3	1	2
Life Expectancy			
1984	2	1	3
1991	2	1	3
1998	2	1	3
2005	2	1	3
2012	2	1	3
2019	2	1	3
2026	2	1	3
Nutrition			
1984	1	2	2
1991	2	1	3
1998	2	1	3
2005	2	1	3
2012	2	1	3
2019	2	1	3
2026	2	1	3

Since cost estimates for typical family planning programmes are unavailable, the Planning simulation is based on a different approach. From World Bank estimates of the cost of training basic community health teams, the number of teams has been calculated for an expenditure equal to the original investment increment. The resulting number has then been divided into the number of females of child-bearing age in each hypothetical country to produce ratios of 'target' females to community health personnel. In no case was the result greater than 200 fertile-age women per three-person team.

Under these assumptions, it seems reasonable to suppose that such an expansion of community health workers would represent an effort equivalent to a Mauldin-Berelson score of at least 3 (their maximum index score is 30). In the African case, a one-period increase of 3 in the M–B index is sufficient to produce a per capita income higher than that produced by the one-period direct investment alternative. In the South American case, an increase of only 2 is sufficient to produce the same effect. The simulation results reported have been generated by these conservatively estimated increases. In view of the apparent possibilities for population coverage associated with resource increments of the magnitude considered, it is entirely possible that the suggested one-period impacts on the family planning index are underestimated. In any case, the intertemporal results for per capita income and the PQLI variables have been included.

The pattern of intertemporal fluctuation in rankings for Africa makes it obvious that any policy conclusions cannot be divorced from explicit valuation of PQLI outcomes, as well as a discount rate. Except for an intermediate period in which the School variant dominates absolutely, there are no clear winners in this experiment. During the first periods, the results of the Investment and School simulations exhibit approximate parity, while the balance shifts from Investment to Planning in later periods. Since the assumptions underlying the Planning simulation may well be too conservative, the balance might be expected to shift sooner than this particular experiment would indicate.

In the South American case, the final judgement can be made with more certainty. In all but the first period, the School result dominates absolutely. Again, however, the same evolutionary pattern is evident in the rankings for the other variants. During the first periods, Investment clearly dominates, but Planning has overtaken it in two categories by the final period.

Certainly, the set of illustrations presented here provides no conclusive evidence concerning the trade-offs which would be confronted by policy-makers in actual cases. Although careful attempts have been made to estimate the parameters of all model equations in appropriate ways, the simulation results are inevitably sensitive to the specifications which have been adopted. In the final analysis, the conclusion which emerges from the simulation seems sensible, however. In brief summary, this conclusion might be stated as follows.

There can be no definitive statements as to which of a set of hypothetical resource allocations is absolutely superior. Initial conditions will create different short-run marginal productivities, and the long-run consequences of alternative policies may well be quite different from their short-run results. In its current form, the simulation model illustrates these lessons without necessarily providing a definite basis for analysis in particular national cases. It is true that the initial conditions for a particular society could be used along with alternative policies for specific predictions. Since the non-availability of appropriate data has greatly handicapped the construction of such models in the past, the predictions yielded by this model could provide a useful basis for discussion concerning apparent future trends. In the final analysis, however, the model in its current form still contains too many simplifications for any great confidence to be placed in its predictions. I will return to a consideration of these simplifications in Part IV.

PART IV

THE POPULATION QUESTION

CHAPTER 8

ON THE TEMPTATION TO ENGAGE IN PROJECTION

The simulation results reported in Part III have a hopeful message: human resource policies can have meaningful impacts on long term socio-economic outcomes. The emphasis thus far has been on the PQLI variables (income, literacy, life expectancy, nutritional adequacy), all of which are scaled in per capita terms. In the international development community, there is also great interest in the denominator in several of these ratios—the size of the population itself.

The model developed in this book has two characteristics which have persuaded me to take a detailed look at the population question. The first is its dynamic structure, which allows it to operate on national data automatically. Since all the equations are specified as differences, the current values taken on by the endogenous variables in the model for a particular country serve as initial conditions for prediction. International cross-section regressions do not have the same capability.

As usual, the existence of a certain technical capability has made the temptation to use it very strong. I confess to having succumbed, and in the following chapters I will use the model to make demographic projections for specific countries and regions. This is admittedly risky. I have been persuaded to plunge ahead by the second characteristic of the model which is of interest in this context—its internal consistency. Like the PQLI projections, the population projections are produced by a full set of structural equations. They therefore allow projected population outcomes to be explicitly related to current policies. This 'structural' approach to demographic projection has obvious conceptual appeal, although many criticisms can certainly be directed at the specific model which I have specified and estimated.

I therefore offer the numbers in the following chapters in the hope that they will stimulate discussion of the structural approach. As will be seen, they are in many ways quite different from the numbers currently offered by the demographic projection services of the United Nations and the World Bank. Wherever possible, I will try to identify the reasons for these differences.

(i) Possible contributions

Veteran demographers whose patience has survived to this point may experience feelings of both resignation and malicious glee upon learning that yet another set of long-term population projections is about to be unveiled. As an outsider, I have the sense that the embarrassing failure to predict the turnaround in Western fertility rates after the Second World War left its mark on demography.[58] Thus, much time in recent years has been devoted to analyses of historical data and to the elaboration of increasingly sophisticated mathematical models, with the dubious task of long-range projection ceded by consensus to a few organizations such as the United Nations and the World Bank.

Certainly, my attempt to use the model presented in this book for long-run projection must seem presumptuous. This is, after all, the work of one person while the published projections of the international statistical agencies represent the collective work of many specialists in many different countries. I recognize that my methodology is more simplistic than the standard approach in some important respects.

Nevertheless, I think that this work has a contribution to make because it incorporates an approach to the statistical analysis of demographic data which has some novel aspects. In the first place, it takes an explicitly structural view of demographic evolution which incorporates both the crude birth-rate and the crude death-rate as long-run endogenous variables. For all but a few attempts at long-run projection, this represents a point of difference. The general practice in country-specific projections is to pre-specify a set of time paths for central tendencies in fertility and mortality which are made to interact with evolving age cohort data to produce population outcomes. It is apparent to everyone, of course, that both fertility and mortality are sensitive to evolving socio-economic conditions, and that this sensitivity can vary over time. Thus, most projections are presented as alternative outcomes which depend on 'optimistic', 'pessimistic', and 'medium' assumptions about the evolution of these two crucial change rates.

The model presented in this book is more specific. The crucial roles in projection are played by the rate of capital accumulation, by social priorities reflected in relative commitments to education, medical care, and family planning, and by the present conditions and recent history of a particular society. Thus, my approach takes one step further back into structural explanation. Rather than pre-specifying time paths for fertility and mortality, I have made them dependent upon a complex series of interactions which depend upon pre-specified paths for educational and medical expansion as well as a whole set of behavioural parameters for the system which have been estimated econometrically. While it is impossible to avoid guesses about the paths taken by some variables in a simulation system unless the entire operation is a degenerate extrapolation using distributed lags (and in such a case it would soon settle to an unrealistic equilibrium state), it seems defensible to argue for an approach which accents the role of variables which can be directly affected by public policy.

Other simulation exercises have, of course, used statistical analyses of fertility and mortality rate determination as bases for projection. Again, however, my research seems to have departed from past precedent in certain ways. The most important of these is undoubtedly the combination of cross section and time series which has been employed in the econometric work. All estimated demographic equations in this book relate changes in fertility and mortality in Third World countries during the past two decades to changes in determining socio-economic variables. Since this approach incorporates substantial within-country experience as well as across-country experience, it may allow for a more realistic view of the impact of causal variables on demographic outcomes.

In this latter connection, an additional departure taken by this study should be noted. Much attention has been paid to the role played by family planning in fertility decline during the past two decades, but I have argued that its true relation with fertility should probably be regarded as simultaneous: family planning programmes are likely to bear the most fruit in soil which is already rich, for whatever reason. Thus, the econometric work and the resulting simulation equations are based on a simultaneous specification of the relationship between family planning and fertility. In this way, I have attempted to arrive at an unbiased estimate of the true impact of family planning on fertility during the recent past.

Although it has already been discussed in great detail, one further facet of the work reported here should be noted. Because this book features a dynamic model of output determination as well as a model of demographic change, it makes possible a simulation model which allows for feedback effects from current population growth to future demographic change rates through various impacts on the output system. The most obvious of these is the direct effect on the evolution of per capita income, which has subsequent impacts on nutrition, literacy, the investment rate, output growth, and back into the evolution of fertility and mortality. An additional delayed impact comes through the impact on the future growth of the labour force, which will in turn have an effect on output growth. The explicit tying together of the output and demographic systems allows for a richness of interaction which would not otherwise be possible. Again, there are precedents for this approach. However, I am not aware of any existing studies which have tied together a consistent set of relations estimated on time changes in the manner introduced by this book.

(ii) Some problems

After making all these claims, I must immediately begin the task of hedging my conclusions. I hope that this book has something to say about population projection. There are, however, several limitations of my modelling approach which should be borne in mind when interpreting my results. I can best illustrate the limitations with a short digression concerning the Limits to Growth and the Population Bomb.[59]

In the dramatic writings of those who predict a dangerous passage for the world during the next century, two monsters of mythic dimension are presumed to guard the straits. Scylla is the unchecked spread of nuclear weapons technology, while the role of Charybdis is played by population growth. The tragedy usually unfolds in a vision of a hundred years war between over-populated, wretchedly poor Third World countries and their First (and Second?) World counterparts. The shadow of Charybdis seems to have fallen over many writings by development specialists, as well.

Ultimately, this concern with sheer numbers of people must come from one of two sources. Because many specialists are still citizens of wealthy societies, part of their unease may stem from the feeling that national power and population are roughly correlated. Most of the worry, however, is undoubtedly less Machiavellian than Malthusian in spirit. During the 1970s, it has again become fashionable to worry that population increase will steadily outpace the growth of output, so that progressive immiseration will be the lot of great numbers in the Third World. It is frequently asserted that poor countries will be unable to accumulate capital at an appropriate pace; that the nature of capital accumulation will be such that labour cannot be absorbed at the requisite pace; or that there are simply resource limitations which will fundamentally apply a brake to the growth of output while population proceeds apace (at least until some ultimate, catastrophic 'readjustment').

I confess to a personal aversion to this kind of pessimism. However, I must admit what has undoubtedly become obvious already to the critical reader. This book does not provide much real ammunition for optimists. In the case of the capital problem, my results are perfectly consistent with the Malthusian vision under the assumption that individual countries maintain low investment rates in the face of falling death-rates and high initial fertility. Although such perverse behaviour has not been widely evident in the Third World to date, some uncomfortable examples do seem to exist.

A fundamental weakness of the present work may well be its treatment of the phenomenon of labour absorption in poor countries. As noted in the chapter on the output model, the Cobb–Douglas form has been employed throughout in the estimation of parameters in the output equations. Since this form builds in unitary elasticity of substitution by assumption, it permits the future absorption of labour in a way which may well be questioned by those who see rising un-employment of labour force entrants as a threat in many poor countries. Although it should be recalled that a linear specification of the CES production function proved to be no better than the Cobb–Douglas, the attendant estimation difficulties were such that the empirical result can scarcely be called conclusive. Unavoidably, then, an am-biguity remains. Any predictions made by the output model employed in this book are bound to be over-optimistic in the view of those who think that the long-run elasticity of substitution between capital and labour is considerably less than one.

My results will also not be believable by those who think that natural resource limitations or environmental capacity problems impose fundamental limits to growth. If these factors are regarded as fixed in the long run, then the result for the world production system must be a progressive deterioration in the productivity of labour and capital as the limits are approached.

Certainly, eloquent voices have been raised in defence of the notion of fundamental, impending limits. Equally eloquent voices have denied the meaningful existence of such limits once technical progress is allowed its due. It is unlikely that this debate will have a conclusion, and it will certainly not occur in the near future. I therefore present my results, while acknowledging that they rest on the implicit assump-tion that no fundamental limits to growth will bind the world system during the period of interest to this study.

In summary, then, the stance reflected by the simulations reported here is as follows: the investment rate for poor countries in the future will continue to behave roughly as it has in the past; capital and labour are easily substitutable for one another in aggregate production through time; and diminishing returns from the effects of environmental and resource constraints will not fundamentally bind the system during the period under study. My results are bound to be questioned by those who reject these assumptions.

One more element needs to be considered here. In this book, I have had little to say about the argument between pro-natalists and family planning advocates. The model does, of course, consider some phe-nomena which bear on this argument, but the interpretation of simula-tion results can probably be used to support either side. At the risk of over-simplification, the pro-natalist position (in so far as it pertains to socio-economic issues) might be summarized in two propositions:

first, an expanding population aids in the expansion of national output by promoting expansion in the labour force, economies of scale, more opportunities for innovation, and (possibly) an increased savings rate.[60] Secondly, to the extent that sheer population size makes a difference in a world whose political dynamics reflect potential military power, rapid population growth may provide an indirect route to enhanced economic power.

Although the second argument is certainly plausible, there is nothing in this study which could be used for either support or rejection. It therefore seems best simply to remain silent on this issue. The more direct forces posited in the first argument, however, are related to the question of model specification and should be considered here. All the econometric estimates which I have obtained support one firm conclusion: the direct impact of the birth-rate on future output growth through expansion in the labour force produces an increment in the numerator of per capita income which is insufficient to outweigh the increment in the denominator.

Although simulation runs with my model do not support the pronatalist argument, then, several other factors would have to be considered before an appropriate judgement could be made. For example, the argument has been advanced that enhanced family size has a positive impact on national savings behaviour because of its impact on the behaviour of household heads. At first glance the latter argument seems paradoxical, since the presence of additional children would seem to provide a powerful stimulus for additional family consumption expenditures. Some pro-natalists have argued, however, that the combined impact of additional available family labour and the necessity of enhanced saving for education, dowries, etc., is sufficient to shift the balance in the other direction. In order to test for this possibility, I re-specified the investment rate equation with the population growth rate as an additional explanatory variable. The sign of the resulting term was positive (which supports the pro-natalist argument), although the parameter estimate was quite diffuse in the full multivariate equation and the 95 per cent confidence interval always included zero and part of the range of negative numbers.

In order to give the pro-natalist argument its full due, I used the positive coefficient in the revised investment rate equation as the maximum likelihood estimate of the population growth effect and re-ran the simulation for a representative set of cases. Again, the ultimate impact on per capita income and the PQLI indices was retarding, although obviously less so than in the simulations which excluded the positive population growth effect from the investment rate equation.

Thus, my results do not seem to support the first pro-natalist argument, either in the intermediate or long run. I would be the first to affirm, however, that a model as simple in structure as mine cannot really be used to test the full range of hypotheses suggested by Simon (1977) and others. My results say nothing, moreover, about the attractiveness of large populations as assets in international politics.

CHAPTER 9

EXISTING METHODOLOGIES

(i) The United Nations projections

Several current programmes provide regular population projections which extend for various periods into the future. Generally, the most publicized predictions are those for the year 2000, as well as those which specify final equilibrium populations for various countries and the approximate years in which these population levels will be reached under the assumptions which have yielded the predictions. Probably the best-known and most widely utilized set of projections is that published by the United Nations.

Periodically, the United Nations publishes a comprehensive set of population projections for all countries in the world. The sources employed for this exercise are rather diverse. For countries which have well-developed demographic services (i.e. the industrialized nations and several nations in Latin America), the tendency is to rely on projections which are furnished by the national statistical services. Since these projections are based on relatively precise local data and on the knowledge of national specialists, the UN demographers are undoubtedly wise to accept this division of labour.

In the case of most Third World nations, however, the UN is forced to rely on its own resources for the projection of future population. Generally, the UN demographers follow a two-part strategy. First, they obtain current estimates of fertility and mortality by age cohort group for each country (or they use 'representative' regional figures for those countries which do not have such data). Obviously, these numbers are extremely rough in many cases. Infant mortality data are often imperfectly kept, and the recording of births in rural societies can be far from comprehensive. In many cases reliable census data are not available, so current estimates of fertility and mortality rates have to be produced using extrapolations from past observations on population groupings.

This first stage of the demographic projection exercise is at least relatively dependable. The second leg is shakier, for it involves prediction of what *will* be as opposed to rough observation of what actually exists. The short term may not be too risky. It has frequently been noted that population projections twenty years into the future are relatively risk-free because almost all those who will bear children during the period in question are currently alive. The accent must be on 'relatively' here, of course, because health factors will still intervene in ways which cannot be precisely determined. In each year, each female in the population will have a survival probability which will be sensitive to the evolution of health care and nutrition. Demographers who want to project future births are initially faced with the task of predicting how many females who are currently children will enter and survive in the reproductive age cohorts during the projection period. Furthermore, they must make some assumption about survival probabilities for females who are moving through the reproductive age cohort at the start of the projection period.

Obviously, then, no projection can be made without some prediction (explicit or implicit) concerning the future evolution of mortality rates by age cohort. Studies of past demographic patterns have suggested that mortality rates have evolved along fairly stable, declining paths. Thus, the most recent comprehensive UN projections are based on two propositions: (1) Life expectancy improvement in all countries follows essentially the same asymptotic time path once modern medical technology has been introduced. Up to and including the age of 70, it is assumed that life expectancy at birth will increase by constant increments (somewhat over two years) every five years. After the age of 70, the rate of improvement is slowed to reflect the presence of an asymptote in the mid-70s. (2) There is a gap in the life expectancy of men and women which favours the latter, and this gap will remain approximately constant.

Once these assumptions have been imposed, cohort-specific mortality rates can be produced with the aid of computers. The problem of fertility rate projection is generally conceded to be more difficult. While it is universally recognized that changing socio-economic circumstances will have an important effect on fertility behaviour, existing projections take them into account only in a fairly impressionistic way. General observation of the historical behaviour of the industrial societies leads to the derivation of certain rough relationships between key socio-economic indicators such as life expectancy, literacy, income, and fertility. The usual practice is to make several educated guesses about future patterns of socio-economic progress for particular regions, and to use these patterns for the generation of 'low', 'medium', and 'high' estimates of fertility decline in the coming years. General patterns are projected at the regional level, and projections for a particular country are essentially tailored to these patterns.

Thus, existing long-run forecasts of population change do contain the results of some attempt to incorporate the relationship between anticipated socio-economic improvements and fertility. None of the existing institutional projection efforts, however, builds upon a

model which is explicit. Thus, it is difficult to judge the relative likelihood of multiple fertility trajectories, and widely different future
populations must be accorded the same legitimacy in the mind of the
uninformed reader.

(ii) Statistical models

While explicit models of socio-economic evolution and fertility change
have not been employed in the world projection projects, there have
been many attempts at statistical analysis of the relationship between
fertility and a set of relevant socio-economic determinants. As always
the most convincing exercises have been at the micro-level. Generally,
survey difficulties have limited such exercises to cross-sectional analysis,
so that the risk of confounding variables is ever present in the interpretation of results. At the international level, data difficulties have
also limited analysts to the consideration of cross-section models.[61]

One of the most ambitious of these cross-section exercises is due
to Dyson, Bell *et al.* (1978), and it serves as a good illustration of the
promises and dangers of this kind of approach. Although the authors
had historical data for certain newly industrialized countries (NICs)
such as Taiwan which might serve as bases for the prediction of general
patterns of fertility evolution in LDCs, they recognized that the available examples did not exhibit sufficient regional diversity to serve as
very reliable guides. They therefore focused attention on cross-section
data, using appropriate functional specifications to fit a model of the
apparent covariation of fertility with mortality and per capita income
across the full international spectrum in the most recent period.

Such cross-sectional evidence can be used as a basis for projection
if individual national data are regarded as random sample draws from
observations created by a common historical process. It is clear that
the application of this assumption to a set of countries bounded by
Rwanda and Sweden may be questionable, to put it mildly. In fact
the risk involved in this kind of exercise is illustrated by the work of
Dyson and his associates, who use reasonable projections of per capita
income growth and mortality decline to project changes in population
for hypothetical LDC examples. Their conclusion, from the cross-
section evidence, is that the expected growth of population is so
great as to seem rather absurd. In the final analysis they lean toward
acceptance of the evidently steeper relationship which have characterized the NICs as a better basis for prediction, while recognizing that
some regional peculiarity may be present.

(iii) Simulation models

In the social sciences, the availability of the digital computer means that the size and sophistication of projection models are not limited by the aggravation of hand calculation. The only real check on the ambition of model builders is their willingness to be constrained by the available data. I have taken a very conservative route by limiting myself to dynamic relations which can be estimated using a consistent international data set. Others have been willing to sacrifice econometric purity for breadth of vision, and the result has been a long tradition of macro-policy simulation. Beginning with the pioneering effort of Coale and Hoover (1958), this tradition runs through the work of Blandy and Wery (1973), Barlow and Davies (1974), and Simon (1977).

As time has passed, these models have become huge. The Barlow-Davies effort, for example, is reported to have contained 1690 equations (many of them 'housekeeping' equations to track the evolution of age cohorts in their demographic submodel). How have the necessary parameters for such detailed models been obtained? Blandy and Wery (1973) have provided a succinct response in their description of the Bachue model sponsored by the ILO:

Bachue-1 is not a representation of any particular country . . . but a representation of an archetypal developing country drawing on a system of theoretical and hypothetical relations quantified on the basis of published research, regression analysis, expert judgment and hunch. (p. 442.)

This eclectic spirit allows simulation modellers essentially free rein in the specification of structural relations governing changes in output, factors of production, human resource investments, fertility, and mortality. The best recent efforts (e.g. Barlow-Davies, Blandy-Wery) provide marvellously detailed depictions of dynamic interactions among many sectors, many production factors, many age cohorts, and many forms of public investment. As I have noted in my introduction to Part III, such models can make a very useful contribution to the construction of full, internally consistent models of the development process. It is not clear whether any of their creators would advocate their use for country-specific projections. None, in any case, has had the temerity to try this on a large scale.

I do not, therefore, regard these efforts as present contenders in the transnational projections game. I have learned a good deal from reading about them, and I eagerly await the time when the available data will allow us to delete 'expert judgment and hunch' from the process of setting their parameter values.

CHAPTER 10

THE FUTURE IN MINIATURE:
ILLUSTRATIONS AND COMPARISONS

The discussion of current approaches to projection in Chapter 9 has been intended to illustrate some problems with existing work. One is the failure of large-scale projects to base their fertility and mortality projections on consistent models of socio-economic evolution which can be critically evaluated. The second is the scarcity of relevant time series data for a large number of countries. This has forced statistical analyses of fertility rate determination to focus on cross-sectional data in a manner which implies that the future of the LDCs is simply the past of the advanced industrial societies. Large-scale simulation models have avoided these problems, but only by abandoning econometrics.

Although many obvious problems remain, the projection work reported in this book is (among other things) an attempt to attack these fundamental difficulties. I should reiterate that this work is offered in a spirit of humility. One researcher cannot hope to do population projections for a large set of countries which match the detail and intricacy of those provided by the demographic services of the international agencies. A close examination of the demographic component of the growth model has undoubtedly made this apparent to specialists. My own feeling is that the simplifications are differences in detail which do not affect the aggregate pattern revealed by the population projections. In any case, I hope that the empirical and theoretical basis for the following projections will be of sufficient interest to stimulate further work of this kind.

Although many strategies could be followed in the presentation of simulation results for actual (as opposed to hypothetical) societies, I will employ the results presented here in three ways. First, I will use some suggestive 'matched pairs' of neighbouring countries to trace the reasons for projected future divergences from existing conditions of rough equivalence. In this way, the basic mechanics of the simulation model itself may be revealed more fully to the reader.

Once this exploratory comparison of paired-country projections has been accomplished, I will turn my attention to a relatively small set of countries which are of major concern because their populations loom so large in the total for the Third World. My list is not exhaustive, but it does seem sufficient to yield some interesting conclusions concerning projected patterns of evolution during the coming decades. The countries which will be used for illustration (in low- medium- and high-variant cases) here are Mexico, Brazil, Nigeria, Egypt, Pakistan, India, Bangladesh, and Indonesia.

My third task will be an attempt at global projection. Ultimately, the dominant question must be the population which the poor regions of the world will be required to sustain. Although the countries just mentioned will determine a major part of the evolving story, it would undoubtedly be a mistake to limit projections to these giants alone. For this reason, projections have also been produced for twenty-eight other LDCs whose historical data were sufficient to provide the initial conditions required for simulation model runs. These countries are scattered across all the poor regions, and although they could scarcely be termed a pure random sample, the collective pattern of evolution by region which they suggest can be regarded as a fairly reliable proxy for the full pattern which would be predicted by the model if sufficient data were available for all countries. In the concluding chapter, this large sample of country projections will be used as a basis for determining the most likely evolution of Third World population, which will in turn be compared with current World Bank projections.

(i) Comparative socio-economic dynamics

In Part III, the behaviour of the simulation model was illustrated with the aid of a set of policy experiments for hypothetical countries which were taken to be representative of particular poor regions. While these illustrations yielded some indication of system sensitivity to shifts in the paths taken by important exogenous variables, they did not provide a very complete illustration of the reasons for this sensitivity.

It might also be argued that the projected paths for the exogenous variables in the first simulation runs were not very realistic. Many LDCs have recently been expanding social services faster than their growth in per capita income would predict. For the projection exercises, I have revised the social service equations to take this into account. The revised model is included in Appendix D. All equations are identical to those in Figure 12 except for (1), (2), (3), (33), and (37). For (1), (2), (33), and (37), I have included LOW, MEDIUM, and HIGH variants to portray varying levels of commitment to human resource investment and capital accumulation.

The MEDIUM variant is based on actual experience during the period 1960–77: primary schooling typically grew by 8 per cent in each seven-year period; the exponent in the medical equation reflects the typical rate of decrease in the ratio of population to doctors during seven-year periods. The LOW and HIGH variants assume effort levels proportionally lower and higher than historical mean values. In the LOW set, schooling expands at half the typical rate and increments in the family planning index are held to half those predicted by the model. The exponent in the medical equation is set at 0.99 rather than 0.9775. The HIGH variant doubles the MEDIUM schooling increase rate; adds 10 (one-third of the maximum level) to the predicted increment in family planning; adds 3 per cent to the predicted investment rate change; and lowers the medical exponent to 0.95.

The LOW and HIGH adjustments to observable trends are substantial. As we shall see in later sections, the consequences of these adjustments seem quite substantial, as well. In this section, the revised model will be introduced through an application of the MEDIUM equations to pairs of countries whose current circumstances are roughly comparable. If the projection model indicates systematic divergences in the future, then an analysis of the reasons may enhance our understanding of the way in which the model seems to be working. For the present purposes, two comparisons will be employed: Kenya v. Tanzania and India v. Pakistan.

(1) *Kenya and Tanzania*

During the 1970s, the comparative experiences of Kenya and Tanzania have frequently been cited in debates concerning the relative merits of different development strategies. Kenya is used (and quite frequently attacked) as an example of capitalist growth, while Tanzania is said to provide an example of socialism with an emphasis on rural development. Although the experiences of the two countries have not been as opposed as ideologically-motivated debators would have us believe, it is certainly true that the two countries have differed significantly in the degree to which their governments have been involved in the operations of their economies.

Although a general feeling seems to prevail that Tanzania has provided more and better social services for its population, the basic statistics do not really support this claim. In 1977, according to the World Bank, Kenya's unadjusted primary and secondary school enrolment ratios were 105 and 13, repectively, while the equivalent ratios for Tanzania were 70 and 3. The Mauldin–Berelson index of family planning activity awards a score of 6 to Kenya and 3 to Tanzania. Finally, the reported ratios of population/doctor for the two nations were 8840 and 18490, respectively,

Thus, the available statistics which can be meaningfully compared suggest an effort at human resource investment in Kenya which is somewhat greater than that of Tanzania. Against the message implied by these numbers, it can legitimately be argued that the Tanzanians have put more emphasis on adult education and the provision of basic health services in rural areas. Certainly, the statistics for the last two decades do not suggest superior performance for Kenya despite a persistent superiority by the measures of education and health provision which are available and internationally comparable. The relevant numbers are displayed in Figure 17.

For Kenya, the measured literacy rate increased from 20 in 1960 to 30 in 1970 and 40 in 1975. The corresponding rates for Tanzania are 10, 28 and 66, respectively. Obviously, the reported increase from 1970 to 1975 for Tanzania is huge. It reflects an intensive adult education effort by the Tanzanian Government, and it is not clear whether the number for 1975 reflects a meaningful, long-term increase in adult literacy or whether a substantial part of the reported increase is transient or a reflection of enthusiasm on the part of programme planners. Since this book has been concerned with the impact of the educational process on productivity, among other things, it is also doubtful whether rapid adult education involves the combination of intellectual training and 'schooling' which provides a significant productivity increment in the long run. In any case, the Tanzanian performance seems at least comparable with that of Kenya when enthusiasm in self-reporting is taken into account.

A consideration of improvements in life expectancy leads to the same conclusion. In 1960, Kenya had a reported life expectancy of 47 years, while the parallel figure for Tanzania was 42 years. During the next 15 years, expectancies increased to 52 and 47, respectively, in 1970, and to 53 and 51 in 1975. Some convergence seems apparent in the 1970s, although again the reported gain of 4 years of life expectancy in 5 calendar years for Tanzania seems questionable. The existing nutrition statistics suggest the same pattern. Kenya began the 1960s with a large apparent lead, but this has been eroded by a pattern of gradual decline (accentuated in the 1970s), coupled with a sizeable reported jump in nutrition for Tanzania in the 1960s and a small decline in the 1970s.

Thus, during the relevant historical period, the available statistics suggest a persistent but narrowing advantage for Kenya in basic indices of the physical quality of life. In per capita income, its advantage has remained relatively unchanged when measured in constant (1960) dollars. Since the reported investment rates for Kenya have been persistently higher (although some pattern of erosion in the advantage is again evident), the full set of reported statistics would seem to be consistent with the basic hypotheses which were tested in the econometric model. In brief, it could be claimed that a measurable

FIGURE 17

Kenya and Tanzania: Recent History and Projections

	PER CAPITA INCOME		LITERACY RATE		LIFE EXPECT- ANCY		CALORIE ADE- QUACY	
	K	T	K	T	K	T	K	T
1960	100	70	20	10	47	42	103	69
1970	128	95	30	28	52	47	98	88
1977	137	111	40	66	53	51	91	86
1998	278	168	67	63	61	60	102	90
2026	767	332	93	72	71	68	122	102
2054	1740	806	100	90	77	74	144	121

	POPULATION		BIRTH-RATE		DEATH- RATE		FAMILY PLAN- NING	
	K	T	K	T	K	T	K	T
1960	8.0	9.9	51	47	19	22	–	–
1970	11.2	12.9	50	47	15	19	–	–
1977	14.5	15.9	51	48	14	16	6	3
1998	26.1	26.4	34	34	8	10	22	11
2026	49.0	48.2	30	27	7	8	30	25
2054	83.1	75.6	26	23	7	7	30	30

	INVESTMENT RATE	
	K	T
1960	29.2	13.4
1970	27.3	21.2
1977	19.3	18.0
1998	22.6	18.2
2026	20.1	17.3
2054	17.7	18.8

superiority in the investment rate for Kenya has been balanced by relatively greater human resource gains for Tanzania during the past two decades. These gains could in turn be traced to a greater emphasis on distributional equity, so that Kenya's measured superiority in schooling and availability of physicians has been balanced by Tanzania's commitment to adult education and the provision of basic health services in rural areas.

It has been necessary to provide this brief summary of apparent past performance as a prelude to the consideration of the projections which the socio-economic growth model provides for the two countries.

These projections provide a good demonstration of the basic explanatory mechanics of the model, and they also demonstrate that the
model in its present form retains a potentially important ambiguity
with respect to the question of equity.

A perusal of the long-run projections for the two countries reveals
that the predicted evolution of the two societies during the next half
century is quite different.[62] Kenya regains its literacy advantage by the
year 2000, while the apparent gap in life expectancy first narrows a
little further and then widens again in the twenty-first century. Kenya's
per capita income moves ahead much more quickly throughout the
projection period, and this is reflected in a steadily widening nutritional
gap between the two countries. Thus, while the model predicts that
both societies will be much better off by all measures of PQLI in the
coming years, it gives a rather decisive nod to Kenya in its evaluation
of relative outcomes.

There appear to be several basic reasons for the projection of relatively superior performance for Kenya. Since it seemed desirable to
preserve some kinds of basic comparability in the national simulations
reported in this book, the trend rates of progress in primary and secondary schooling and medical personnel availability have been estimated
for the recent past and simply extrapolated to the relevant asymptotic
figure for each country (e.g. a secondary school enrolment figure of
100). Thus, all of the roots of future predicted behaviour can be found
in current data for the two countries.

Four numbers appear to have particular significance for the projection outcomes: the investment rate, the primary school enrolment
ratio, the secondary school enrolment ratio, and the ratio of population
to doctors. The combination of a higher initial investment rate and a
substantially higher primary enrolment ratio promotes a simultaneous,
rapid expansion of literacy and output, the latter being additionally
stimulated by enhanced labour productivity. Both factors enter into
the determination of investment changes, as well, and the positive
feedback effect in this case seems sufficient to modify the forces promoting regression toward the international mean investment rate for
a relatively long period.

While Kenya's advantage in investment and primary schooling
promotes a strong source of relative growth in the output model, its
superior measures for secondary school enrolment and the availability
of doctors have an impact on demographic developments. Kenya's
lower ratio of population to doctors assures that its death-rate continues to fall rapidly, despite the fact that its lower initial level is
closer to the implicit lower limit to begin with. This drop in the death-
rate in turn promotes some fertility rate decline, as families begin

adjusting to the perception of higher survival probability for their children. In the reduction of fertility, the decline in the death-rate is joined by the relatively rapid expansion of income determined by output dynamics.

While both the factors mentioned above are undoubtedly important in the determination of fertility decline, they are matched in significance by a projected expansion in family planning activity which is considerably greater in the Kenyan case. Again, the underlying causes are fairly clear. Fertility change and the expansion of family planning activity are determined simultaneously in the demographic model, so that it is most helpful to think about the reduced form equations. Changes in both per capita income and the death-rate enter into the determination of fertility, and thus into the evolution of family planning activity. At the same time, the secondary school enrolment ratio enters directly into the determination of family planning change. Here, a clear Kenyan advantage is apparent. Although neither country could exactly be credited with a spectacular commitment to secondary schooling during the 1970s, a ratio of 13 is undeniably better than a ratio of 3.

Thus, the combined effect of three factors generates a predicted increase in family planning activity and a simultaneous fertility decline which are substantially greater in Kenya than in Tanzania during the last quarter of the twentieth century. The predicted Kenyan birth-rate drops from 51 in 1977 to 34 in 1998, while the Tanzanian birth-rate falls from 48 to 34. The predicted change in the Mauldin–Berelson index is from 6 to 22 for Kenya and from 3 to 11 for Tanzania.

Despite the apparent strength of the factors determining fertility change in Kenya, the subsequent projections for the two sets of birth-rates return the advantage to Tanzania. Thus, by 2026, the two birth-rates are predicted to be 30 and 26, respectively, while by 2054 they are projected to have declined to 26 and 23. Not only is a regained advantage for Tanzania apparent here, but a substantial slowing in the pace of birth-rate decline is evident in both countries during the first quarter of the twenty-first century.

Again, the reason for this reduction in birth-rate responsiveness is not difficult to find. By the year 1998, both Kenya and Tanzania are living the consequences of high fertility and low mortality in the mid-1970s. An expanded cohort passes through the years of prime fecundity, and the result is a moderation in the decline of the birth-rate (children born/population) even though the fertility rate continues to drop rapidly. The impact of the age cohort phenomenon is somewhat lessened in Tanzania by a set of factors which determine a relatively rapid expansion of family planning activity during the critical period, and by its lower birth-rate in the 1970s. After this slowing early in the next century, both Kenya and Tanzania are projected to continue experiencing birth-rate decline at a steady, albeit reduced, pace.

For Kenya and Tanzania, then, the demographic dynamics remain pitched slightly in favour of the latter, in spite of a rapid decline in projected Kenyan fertility in the late twentieth century. In every year of the projection, Tanzania's population growth rate (birth-rate — death-rate) is lower than Kenya's. In the very long run, this relative advantage begins to tell for Tanzania. During the last quarter century of the simulation, the cumulative effect of lower population growth is reflected in faster precentage changes in all four of the PQLI indices (income, literacy, life expectancy, nutrition) as it works its way through per capita income. By the end of the simulation period, the Tanzanian investment rate has also risen past that of Kenya.

Thus, the contrasting projected experiences for Tanzania and Kenya provide some insight into the major forces which seem to be built into the economic and demographic equations of the model. In the short and intermediate run (where these are defined in decades), Kenya's initial advantage in investment rate, human resource promotion, and family planning activity give it an evident dynamic advantage. After about fifty years, however, this advantage begins to be eroded for two major reasons. First, the effect of a persistently higher rate of population growth begins to tell. Secondly, several of its important 'sources of growth' (as measured by the model) have lost any further propulsive power by 2026. Kenya has become effectively 100 per cent literate, its life expectancy is approaching the asymptote, and family planning activity has reached a relatively complete state. In addition, the death-rate has moved into a balance determined by declining numbers of high-risk children and rising numbers of high-risk older adults.

Once all the socio-demographic factors have approached their asymptotic levels, the only dynamic multiplier which remains operative in the model is the investment rate. Through its effect on income and fertility, this rate continues to move the society toward higher PQLI levels. However, the absence of any additional stimulation from the human resource variables makes investment-rate change insufficient to overcome the forces promoting regression toward the international mean in the investment rate. By the middle of the next century, the Kenyan investment rate is dropping back slightly in response to this force. Tanzania, on the other hand, has not yet reached some of the socio-economic asymptotes and is therefore propelled ahead more quickly than Kenya during the latter simulation periods.

As a conclusion to this comparative exercise, I should point out that it remains an application of *'ceteris paribus'* reasoning for all its complexity. It ignores the possibility of technical progress beyond the impact of basic human resource formation and therefore does not allow for the phenomenon which has continued to propel the advanced industrial societies. Since it is purely a closed model, it does not take into account the role of international economic flows in the formation of capital and the stimulation of productivity.[63] A third weakness has already been mentioned: the model is not designed to take the effect of redistributive strategies into account, except in so far as these strategies have an impact on comparable indices such as schooling, medical care, and family planning activity. As I have argued in my discussion of the data employed for this study, group averages such as life expectancy, literacy, and nutritional adequacy must be at least fair indicators of general welfare levels. Nevertheless, the absence of data appropriate for explicit comparison of the impact of redistribution prevented the incorporation of public commitment to equity as part of the model.

(2) *India and Pakistan*

While a consideration of projections for India and Pakistan provides some additional dramatic examples of the impact of human resource commitments on socio-economic outcomes, a full consideration of the relative dynamics in this case would involve repetition of the Kenya–Tanzania discussion. For this reason, I will content myself with highlighting the major differences in long-run performance suggested by the simulations, as well as the apparent reasons for these differences.

In a consideration of the familiar indices of general welfare, the statistics for India and Pakistan in the mid-1970s suggest no clear winner (see Figure 18). Pakistan's per capita income and nutritional sufficiency measures are higher, the countries have the same measured life expectancy, and India has a higher literacy rate. However, the Kenya–Tanzania case has clearly demonstrated the importance of the indices of current commitment to investment in physical capital, human resources, and family planning in determining long-run outcomes. Here, the statistics suggest that India has a strong and consistent superiority. During the 1970s, India's investment rate has been substantially higher than Pakistan's. In the mid-1970s, its primary school enrolment ratio, secondary school ratio, and population/doctor ratio were all superior (79–50, 26–17, and 3140–3780, respectively). Finally, India has expanded its family planning activity at a considerably quicker pace than has Pakistan. The results of the differences in policy for the two countries may already be apparent in their differential

FIGURE 18
India and Pakistan: Recent History and Projections

	PER CAPITA INCOME		LITERACY RATE		LIFE EXPECT- ANCY		CALORIE ADE- QUACY	
	I	P	I	P	I	P	I	P
1960	60	60	28	15	43	44	95	84
1970	70	91	33	20	48	48	92	94
1977	75	96	36	21	51	51	89	93
1998	150	144	52	32	59	56	95	92
2026	390	306	70	47	67	63	109	103
2054	1083	703	87	63	73	68	129	120

	POPULATION		BIRTH-RATE		DEATH- RATE		FAMILY PLAN- NING	
	I	P	I	P	I	P	I	P
1960	436.2	45.4	43	49	21	23	–	–
1970	547.6	59.8	40	47	17	18	–	–
1977	633.3	74.0	35	45	14	15	19	8
1998	877.1	121.4	22	31	8	9	30	26
2026	1214.2	211.4	16	27	8	7	30	30
2054	1434.8	331.6	12	22	8	7	30	30

	INVESTMENT RATE	
	I	P
1960	15.3	12.5
1970	17.9	15.8
1977	19.8	11.9
1998	19.9	17.7
2026	19.3	17.6
2054	19.3	18.4

fertility decline. While India's measured birth-rate fell from 43 to 35 during the period 1960–77, Pakistan experienced a decline from 49 to 45.

As the two countries stand poised at the beginning of the simulation period, then, the outstanding facts are as follows: India has a substantially higher rate of physical capital formation, a substantially higher commitment to primary and secondary schooling, and a lower population growth rate. Since all relevant indicators point in the same direction, the implication is clear: we would expect the projections to show India surging ahead in the standard PQLI measures.

Obviously, the results confirm our intuition. By the final projection year (2054), India is substantially ahead of Pakistan in per capita income, literacy, life expectancy, and nutrition. Furthermore, its birth-rate decline has continued at such a substantial rate that the differential for the two societies is maintained. India's projected human-resource progress into the next century is sufficient to forestall much downard pressure on its investment rate throughout the simulation. During the latter part of the simulation period, India's death-rate becomes slightly higher than that of Pakistan as its population progressively ages.

Since the mechanics underlying these projections have been discussed in the Kenya-Tanzania case, only a few additional comments seem appropriate at this point. The most significant feature its probably the optimistic portrayal of future Indian experience. In the past, India has frequently been used as the hopeless foil in international socio-economic comparisons. The simulation results suggest, however, that a substantial commitment to investment, family planning, and human resources by India during the past decade may be ushering it into an era of demonstrable rewards. Although the predicted per capita income for India several decades hence is certainly not royal, it represents an average level of living vastly more comfortable than that dictated by present circumstances. For the PQLI indices, the projection for mid-twenty-first-century India suggests a lifestyle which is tolerable indeed.

Perhaps the most dramatic projection in the case of India is the continued decrease in the rate of population growth. By the middle of the next century, India's projected population is only somewhat more than twice the present level. The prospect of 1.4 billion people on the subcontinent is not altogether reassuring, to be sure, but this projection appears to be substantially below that of most international demographic agencies at present.

The projection for Pakistan is obviously quite different. Pakistan's anticipated commitment to family planning shows a steady increase for the next several decades, and its projected investment rate is somewhat higher than in the immediate past. Nevertheless, the legacy of high birth-rates in the 1970s persists into the next century as large new cohorts bear sufficient children (even at reduced fertility rates) to prevent the kind of rapid birth-rate decline evident in the Indian case. As a result, Pakistan's projected population by the end of the simulation period is greatly expanded and is, clearly, at least several decades from equilibrium.

In considering the phenomenon of relative population growth and economic growth for India and Pakistan, it is impossible to avoid the natalist controversy when drawing a conclusion. When outcomes are

scaled in per capita terms, India's dynamic advantage is striking. However, a consideration of the outcomes in aggregate terms may diminish
this superiority from the pro-natalist perspective. In 1977, the total
income of Pakistan is measured as 15 per cent of India's. In the year
2054, the corresponding percentage is still 15 because Pakistan's population growth has compensated for its slower growth in per capita income. In terms of sheer population size, the shift in favour of Pakistan
is striking. From a 1977 size advantage of 8.6/1, India's relative position has declined to 4.3/1 by the middle of the next century. From
the political perspective of Pakistan, such a shift may not be totally
undesirable.

As usual, then, the consideration of a set of mechanical projections
does not permit value judgements to be escaped. The majority of
readers may well conclude that the Indian outcomes are superior
to those of Pakistan, and that enhanced Indian commitments to family
planning and human resource formation are therefore amply justified
by future expectations. Pro-natalists, however, (and particularly those
from Pakistan) might draw very different conclusions from the same
evidence.

(ii) Population trends to the mid-twenty-first-century: possibilities for the regional giants

The four illustrative cases in the preceding section have been useful
for discerning basic model dynamics and considering the relative
strength of various causal variables in determining long-run outcomes
(at least in so far as these are indexed by econometric measures of
recent historical experience in LDCs). The projections suggest that
current policies can have very pronounced effects on long-run population behaviour, although it is difficult to generalize from such a limited
sample. For this reason, it may be useful to consider a series of projections for the 'population giants'—those countries whose size is
dominant in their own regions. Since the future size of population in
the Third World will be largely determined by the evolution of these
dominant countries in any case, a consideration of their hypothetical
futures is of independent interest.

Eight countries have been selected for study in this section. Mexico
and Brazil have been selected because they clearly dominate Middle
and South America, respectively. From Sub-Saharan Africa, Nigeria
has been selected, while Egypt is the Middle Eastern representative.
From South Asia, Pakistan, India, and Bangladesh are all of sufficient
size to warrant inclusion. Finally, Indonesia has been drawn from South-
East Asia. Unfortunately, China had to be omitted. The simulation

FIGURE 19
Comparative Demographic Projections: Eight Major Nations

(WH = my own simulations (medium case); UN = UN projections (medium case))

MEXICO

	1970	1975	1980	1985	1990	1995
Birth-rate						
(1) UN	42.0	41.7	41.1	39.5	37.3	35.2
(2) WH	42.0	39.1	35.7	32.2	29.9	27.2
(2) – (1)	0.0	–2.6	–5.4	–7.3	–7.4	–8.0
Death-rate						
(1) UN	9.0	7.8	6.9	6.2	5.7	5.2
(2) WH	9.0	8.3	7.9	7.6	7.4	7.1
(2) – (1)	0.0	0.5	1.0	1.4	1.7	1.9
Population Growth Rate						
(1) UN	3.30	3.39	3.42	3.33	3.16	3.00
(2) WH	3.30	3.08	2.78	2.46	2.25	2.01
(2) – (1)	0.0	–.3	–.6	–.9	–.9	–1.0

Population (millions)

	1970	1975	1980	1985	1990	1995	2000
(1) UN	50.3	59.2	70.0	82.8	97.6	114.1	132.2
(2) WH	50.4	59.6	68.8	78.1	87.4	97.0	106.5
(2) – (1)	.1	.4	–1.2	–4.7	–10.2	–17.1	–25.7

BRAZIL

	1970	1975	1980	1985	1990	1995
Birth-rate						
(1) UN	37.1	36.0	34.5	32.9	31.2	29.4
(2) WH	38.0	36.6	33.3	29.3	27.0	23.7
(2) – (1)	.9	.6	–1.2	–3.6	–4.2	–5.7
Death-rate						
(1) UN	8.8	7.8	7.0	6.3	5.7	5.3
(2) WH	9.0	9.0	8.6	8.1	8.1	7.6
(2) – (1)	.2	1.2	1.6	1.8	2.4	2.3
Population Growth Rate						
(1) UN	2.83	2.82	2.75	2.66	2.55	2.41
(2) WH	2.90	2.76	2.47	2.12	1.89	1.61
(2) – (1)	.1	–.1	–.3	–.5	–.7	–.8

Figure 19 (*cont.*)

Population (millions)

	1970	1975	1980	1985	1990	1995	2000
(1) UN	95.2	109.7	126.4	145.1	165.8	188.3	212.5
(2) WH	92.8	107.5	122.3	137.0	151.2	165.1	178.3
(2) − (1)	−2.4	−2.2	−4.1	−8.1	−14.6	−23.2	−34.2

NIGERIA

	1970	1975	1980	1985	1990	1995
Birth-rate						
(1) UN		49.3	49.2	48.9	47.7	46.4	44.8
(2) WH		51.0	51.0	46.8	40.6	37.9	35.0
(2) − (1)|	1.7	1.8	−2.1	−7.1	−8.5	−9.8
Death-rate						
(1) UN		22.7	20.7	18.8	16.9	15.1	13.4
(2) WH		21.0	18.9	17.0	15.3	13.7	11.8
(2) − (1)|	−1.7	−1.8	−1.8	−1.6	−1.4	−1.6
Population Growth Rate						
(1) UN		2.66	2.85	3.01	3.08	3.13	3.14
(2) WH		3.00	3.21	2.98	2.53	2.42	2.32
(2) − (1)|	.3	.4	−.03	−.5	−.7	−.8

Population (millions)

	1970	1975	1980	1985	1990	1995	2000
(1) UN	55.1	62.9	72.6	84.4	98.5	115.3	134.9
(2) WH	66.2	75.7	86.6	98.9	110.7	123.4	136.9
(2) − (1)	11.1	12.6	14.0	14.5	12.2	8.1	2.0

EYGPT

	1970	1975	1980	1985	1990	1995
Birth rate						
(1) UN	37.8	35.5	33.7	31.8	29.9	28.3
(2) WH	40.0	37.1	32.2	26.5	23.3	20.4
(2) − (1)	2.2	1.6	−1.5	−5.3	−6.6	−7.9
Death-rate						
(1) UN	14.0	12.4	11.1	10.0	9.0	8.3
(2) WH	15.0	13.6	11.9	10.4	9.8	8.6
(2) − (1)	1.0	1.2	.8	.4	.8	.3

Figure 19 (*cont.*)

Population Growth Rate

(1) UN		2.38	2.31	2.26	2.18	2.09	2.00
(2) WH		2.50	2.35	2.03	1.61	1.35	1.18
(2) − (1)		.1	.05	−.2	−.6	−.7	−.8

Population (millions)

	1970	1975	1980	1985	1990	1995	2000
(1) UN	33.3	37.5	42.1	47.2	52.6	58.4	64.6
(2) WH	33.3	37.2	41.4	45.5	49.2	52.4	55.4
(2) − (1)	0.0	−.3	−.7	−1.7	−3.4	−6.0	−9.2

PAKISTAN

	1970	1975	1980	1985	1990	1995

Birth-rate

	1970	1975	1980	1985	1990	1995
(1) UN	47.4	46.8	44.4	40.8	36.5	32.5
(2) WH	47.0	45.6	42.0	37.6	35.4	32.4
(2) − (1)	−.4	−1.2	−2.4	−3.2	−1.1	−.1

Death-rate

	1970	1975	1980	1985	1990	1995
(1) UN	16.5	14.5	12.5	10.7	9.1	7.8
(2) WH	18.0	15.9	13.9	12.2	10.9	9.5
(2) − (1)	1.5	1.4	1.4	1.5	1.8	1.7

Population Growth Rate

	1970	1975	1980	1985	1990	1995
(1) UN	3.09	3.23	3.19	3.01	2.74	2.47
(2) WH	2.90	2.97	2.81	2.54	2.45	2.29
(2) − (1)	−.2	−.3	−.4	−.5	−.3	−.2

Population (millions)

	1970	1975	1980	1985	1990	1995	2000
(1) UN	60.4	70.6	83.0	97.4	113.2	129.9	146.9
(2) WH	59.8	69.9	80.4	91.1	102.1	114.1	126.6
(2) − (1)	−.6	−.7	−2.6	−6.3	−11.1	−15.8	−20.3

INDIA

	1970	1975	1980	1985	1990	1995

Birth-rate

	1970	1975	1980	1985	1990	1995
(1) UN	39.9	38.7	36.2	33.3	29.9	26.3
(2) WH	40.0	36.4	31.9	27.2	24.7	22.7
(2) − (1)	.1	−2.3	−4.3	−6.1	−5.2	−3.6

Figure 19 (cont.)

Death-rate

(1) UN		15.7	13.9	12.2	10.8	9.6	8.7
(2) WH		17.0	14.9	13.0	11.5	10.4	9.2
(2) − (1)		1.3	1.0	.8	.7	.8	.5

Population Growth Rate

(1) UN		2.42	2.48	2.40	2.25	2.03	1.76
(2) WH		2.30	2.15	1.89	1.57	1.43	1.35
(2) − (1)		−.1	−.3	−.5	−.7	−.6	−.4

Population (millions)

	1970	1975	1980	1985	1990	1995	2000
(1) UN	543.1	613.2	694.3	782.9	876.1	969.7	1059.4
(2) WH	547.6	608.8	671.6	733.8	789.6	844.4	899.5
(2) − (1)	4.5	−4.4	−22.7	−49.1	−86.5	−125.3	−159.9

BANGLADESH

	1970	1975	1980	1985	1990	1995

Birth-rate

	1970	1975	1980	1985	1990	1995
(1) UN	49.5	49.7	48.1	44.9	40.7	36.4
(2) WH	48.0	46.6	42.7	38.0	35.7	32.0
(2) − (1)	−1.5	−3.1	−5.4	−6.9	−5.0	−4.4

Death-rate

	1970	1975	1980	1985	1990	1995
(1) UN	22.1	21.8	19.2	17.0	14.8	12.8
(2) WH	20.0	18.6	16.3	13.8	13.0	11.0
(2) − (1)	−2.1	−3.2	−2.9	−3.2	−1.8	−1.8

Population Growth Rate

	1970	1975	1980	1985	1990	1995
(1) UN	2.74	2.79	2.89	2.79	2.59	2.36
(2) WH	2.80	2.80	2.64	2.42	2.27	2.10
(2) − (1)	.1	.01	−.2	−.4	−.3	−.3

Population (millions)

	1970	1975	1980	1985	1990	1995	2000
(1) UN	67.7	73.7	84.8	98.0	112.1	128.3	144.3
(2) WH	70.8	80.4	90.9	102.1	113.8	126.2	139.0
(2) − (1)	3.1	6.7	6.1	4.1	1.1	−2.1	−5.3

Figure 19 (cont.)

	INDONESIA						
	1970	1975	1980	1985	1990	1995	
Birth-rate							
(1) UN	42.9	40.9	38.1	34.2	30.6	26.7	
(2) WH	43.0	38.7	33.5	28.3	25.6	22.6	
(2) − (1)	.1	−2.2	−4.6	−5.9	−5.0	−4.1	
Death-rate							
(1) UN	16.9	15.0	13.2	11.6	10.2	9.2	
(2) WH	18.0	16.6	14.8	13.1	12.2	10.7	
(2) − (1)	1.1	1.6	1.6	1.5	2.0	1.5	
Population Growth Rate							
(1) UN		2.60	2.59	2.49	2.26	2.04	1.75
(2) WH		2.50	2.21	1.87	1.52	1.34	1.19
(2) − (1)		−.1	−.4	−.6	−.7	−.7	−.5

Population (millions)							
	1970	1975	1980	1985	1990	1995	2000
(1) UN	119.5	136.0	154.9	175.5	196.6	217.6	237.5
(2) WH	117.6	128.7	141.2	154.2	165.4	176.2	186.5
(2) − (1)	−1.9	−7.3	−13.7	−21.3	−31.2	−41.4	−51.0

model has very substantial requirements for data on initial conditions and data on immediate past trends. The available data for China are so scanty that extreme improvisation would have been necessary in attempting projections.

Most of the necessary data for the other countries are available. For Brazil, Pakistan, India, Bangladesh, and Indonesia, all the data are present. In the case of Mexico, Nigeria, and Egypt, the population/ physician ratio for the mid-1970s had to be extrapolated from the trend between 1960 and 1970. Nigeria's literacy rate in the mid-1970s also had to be extrapolated from earlier observations.

Since it is instructive to consider the wider implications of my approach to socio-demographic modelling, I will use the regional giants as the basis for comparing some standard projections with my own. My principal 'foil' will be the intermediate-run population projections completed by the United Nations in 1973.[64] I regret that more recent projections were not available to me at the time of writing since my own model benefited from the use of data through 1977. I will attempt to compensate by including the most recent World Bank projections of ultimate population size. These projections are good for comparison, since they represent an updated application of methods similar to those of the UN.

As a preface to a discussion of the differences in projection and their possible significance, contrasting demographic projections through the year 2000 are presented in Figure 19. These projections allow for identification of the origin of the differences by considering original population estimates, crude birth-rates, and crude death-rates. Once the resulting patterns have been analysed, the next chapter will compare my projections of ultimate population size to the current (1980) projections of the World Bank.

In gross summary, the differences between the UN (medium-variant) projections for the eight countries and my own can be stated as follows: both sets of projections anticipate birth-rates for all countries which are substantially lower in 2000 than in 1970. It is clear, however, that the pattern of projected decline is different for several countries in the set. In all cases, my birth-rate projections are below those of the UN beyond 1980. The figures for 1970 and 1975 have been included to support two fundamental points. The initial World Bank estimates with which I worked are somewhat different from their UN counterparts, as the pattern of random variation in the 1970 column suggests. The 1975 estimates show the beginnings of a rather systematic divergence, however.

It is this second column of birth-rate data which may well hold the key to understanding the substantial difference in the two sets of projections. Although the demographic statistics for the UN are drawn from a 1977 publication, they represent calculations which were actually done in 1973. My 1975 estimate, however, represents an interpolation between World Bank estimates for the years 1970 and 1977. Clearly, something happened in the 1970s which was not readily apparent to UN demographers when they examined data for the first year or two of the decade. With the exception of Nigeria, all my estimates for 1975 are below the corresponding UN projections.

As subsequent columns reveal, the divergence between the two sets of estimates grows, well into the 1980s, for all countries, and only begins reconverging for some during the latter part of the 1980s. Generally, this pattern of divergence is due to a difference in the timing of the pattern of decline in the birth-rate. The UN projections anticipate gradual rates of decline for most countries through the mid-1980s, with progressive steepening thereafter. Even this steepening is not very pronounced for Mexico, Brazil, and Nigeria, while it is pronounced for the South and South-East Asian countries (Pakistan, India, Bangladesh, and Indonesia). My projections on the other hand, are much more strongly logistic for the next twenty years.

While there are important differences in birth-rate projections for the two sets, no such divergence is evident in the death-rate numbers. Although there is some initial difference in death-rate estimates, the pattern of projected decline during the next two decades is quite similar. My projections for Brazil and Mexico are somewhat more pessimistic in the sense that the projected death-rates in the year 2000 are higher, but otherwise there does not seem to be any discernible pattern to the differences between the two sets.

This rough similarity of death-rate projections is, in fact, not very surprising. The econometric evidence considered in an earlier chapter suggested a strong secular trend at work in the determination of death-rates across all countries in the sample. The implication is that the world-wide diffusion of basic medical technology has produced a steady decline in death-rates which is not highly correlated with changes in many of the variables which might be considered determinants of the process. Both my own projections and those of the UN incorporate the same secular trend, so that the similarity in predictions is not surprising. My death-rate estimates are generally a little higher than those of the UN for the 1970s, and this difference persists in the final estimates. Clearly, however, the differences are so small as to be unimportant when compared with those in the birth-rate projections.

Since my birth-rate estimates are persistently (and often increasingly) lower than those of the UN and my death-rate estimates are generally higher, the conclusion for differential rates of population growth is clear: my own projections are smaller. In the Latin American and African cases, the difference in projections grows from 1980 to 2000. For South and South-East Asia, on the other hand, the projected differences are either stable or declining during the next two decades.

In all cases except that of Nigeria, the result is a growing difference in projected population size. The Nigerian case is anomalous only in the sense that the initial population sizes are very different. While my initial estimate for Nigeria's population is much larger than that used by the UN for these projections, the trend is the same as that observed for the other countries. My growth projection for Nigeria is smaller, and by the year 2000 the two population projections have practically converged.

The consequence of the difference in growth rate estimates for the eight large countries in this sample becomes quite striking by the projection year 2000. For 1970, my estimated total population for the eight countries (1038.5 million) is 13.9 million greater than that of the UN. By the year 2000, on the other hand, my estimate is 303.6 million lower. If the UN projections are used as the base for calculation, this represents a reduction of 28 per cent in estimated population increase for the eight from 1970 to 2000.

From the perspective of those to whom population limitation seems like a good idea, these results must seem cheering indeed. They suggest that the general rate of population growth may taper off more quickly than has previously been predicted. However, all previous admonitions against the 'black box' mentality must come into play at this point. Rather than simply accepting my projections as another more optimistic guess concerning population growth trends, it is important to identify the reasons for the divergence.

As previously noted, the UN projections are essentially driven by patterns of projected fertility decline which are imposed exogenously. While it is true that these patterns are based on some implicit notions concerning the relationship between socio-economic change and demographic change in the long run, there has to date been no attempt to use statistical modelling as a way of making the hypothesized relations explicit. The UN projections allow for uncertainty by including low, medium, and high variants which reflect different time-phasing in the hypothesized pattern of fertility rate decline.

The basis for my own projections is quite different. They are all the results of simulations which have been performed on equations whose parameters have been fitted econometrically to data on changes during the period 1960-77. The only truly exogenous variables in the model as specified are the primary school enrolment ratio, the secondary school enrolment ratio, and the ratio of population to doctors. Many other variables are predetermined in particular time periods, of course, but these three are the only ones whose predicted future behaviour involves anything other than lagged adjustment processes.

For my medium-variant projections, all three exogenous variables have simply been allowed to grow at the rate which characterized the full set of sample countries during the period 1970-77. My high-variant projections have been produced by increasing rates of change substantially, and adding exogenous increase terms to the investment rate and family planning activity. For the low variant, family planning is constrained to grow at only half its predicted rate, and the rates of change in schooling and population to doctor ratios are slowed considerably. The numbers in Figure 19 are drawn from my medium variant projections.

Although the truly exogenous variables are thus relatively few in number, it is clear that they join with a very large number of initial levels and previous changes in determining fundamental growth dynamics for many years after the first year of any simulation exercise. As the accompanying tables have indicated, my projections depart significantly from those of the UN. The time plots suggest that two principal reasons for this departure exist. The first is simply the virtue of hindsight, since fertility rates for many countries dropped more quickly than expected in the 1970s. For the 1980s, therefore, my projected declines in birth-rate simply begin at rates much lower than those of the UN.

The second reason is that my projected drop in birth-rates continues to be sharper. Why the observable steep slide in birth-rates for most of the eight countries? Since the econometric model for the joint determination of fertility rates and family planning activity is not complicated, it should be possible to trace the basic reasons without great difficulty. At the outset, it is worth while to recall that the determinants of changes in the general fertility rate are changes in per capita income, the death-rate, family planning activity, and the age structure of the female population. Change in family planning activity, on the other hand, is determined by the availability of cadres as indexed by the secondary school enrolment ratio and the simultaneous change in the fertility rate.

Obviously the reasons for the projected logistic shape of birth-rate decline must be found in the set of predetermined variables mentioned above. Two candidates appear particularly worthy of consideration. For all sample countries, the anticipated rate of decline in the death-rate is quite rapid down to the level of seven or eight per thousand, at which point some asymptotic behaviour becomes apparent. The relationship between survival probability and childbearing has already been discussed, and the econometric results have suggested a strong effect of declining death-rates on fertility rates over fairly long periods. Since the next two decades are projected to have strongly declining death-rates for some of the eight countries, this is one obvious source of the rapid decline in fertility.

The death-rate projections cannot be the sole determining factor, however. Nations such as Brazil and Mexico which already have relatively low death-rates are also projected to have rapidly declining birth-rates during the next two decades. This leads us to the second logical candidate for consideration, which is the anticipated level of family planning activity. The econometric results have suggested strongly that general training levels and institutional capacity as indexed by the secondary school enrolment ratio have a considerable impact on the ability of countries to undertake large-scale family planning programmes. Such a finding is, of course, completely in accord with common sense. For the demographic projections, the implication is that family planning scores for particular countries will start increasing substantially as a well-developed secondary education structure begins appearing. In countries such as Brazil and India where secondary education is relatively well developed, the model predicts a rapid expansion of efforts to encourage family planning to the maximum Mauldin–Berelson score. In countries with lower secondary schooling ratios such as Nigeria and Bangladesh, progress in family planning is stretched out over longer periods.

While the death-rate, the secondary school enrolment ratio, and family planning activity are certainly important sources of anticipated fertility decline, it would be a mistake to ignore the influence of the other two predetermined variables as well. Those countries which experience higher projected rates of per capita income expansion exhibit differentially steeper rates of fertility decline. At the same time, the age cohort effect can be seen in the pattern of fluctuation around long-run trends. Where high initial birth-rates produce relatively large female cohorts, there is an important secondary effect which appears in later years as the expanded cohort enters the period of peak fertility. Even under conditions of rapid decline in the general fertility rate, the presence of so many prime-age women in the population can cause a substantial slowing in the rate of decline of the birth-rate for a long period. This trend is particularly apparent for countries like Pakistan and Bangladesh, where the high birth-rate in the 1960s produces a strong inflection in the downward trend of the birth-rate during the last two decades of the century.

In the final analysis, then, the differences between my projections and those produced by the UN can be traced to a handful of primary factors. Since my initial simulations contain observations for the 1970s, they incorporate stronger initial downward trends and lower birth-rates than those which generally characterize the UN projections. At the same time, my econometric work indicates that both declining death-rates and rising family planning levels (both in turn influenced by the continuing process of human resource development) have a substantial impact on fertility. Thus my birth-rate projections are more steeply logistic in the twentieth century, incorporating a lengthy period when the trend is strongly downward under this dual stimulus.

This latter difference undoubtedly has one additional source. Although the UN projections allow for cohort-specific fertility behaviour to change over time, they incorporate this phenomenon only into the fertility of new cohorts. Thus, once a cohort has entered the child-bearing years, its adjusted fertility rate is frozen except for proportional shifts which are attributed to age changes. In my projections, on the other hand, socio-economic changes are modelled as affecting all cohorts at the same time. Thus, impacts are generally felt more profoundly in my projections than in those of the UN. As I reported in the chapter on the econometrics of fertility rate determination, the use of the standard format for multiple-constraint testing leads to a resounding failure to reject the hypothesis that cohort-specific general fertility rates are equally affected by socio-economic changes. Thus, my simulation model equation seems consistent with recent historical data in allowing for a generalized impact.

CHAPTER 11

WHERE IT MIGHT END: SOME ILLUSTRATIONS

The numbers in Chapter 10 indicate that by the late 1970s fertility decline in many LDCs had steepened sufficiently for UN projections made half a decade before to begin to fray noticeably. At least one lesson is clear: population projection, even in the intermediate run, is a risky business. Since this lesson has been repeated many times in the past, the most stable prediction we can probably make is that it will be repeated in the future. At the risk of contributing to the fulfilment of this prediction, I now propose to take the final plunge. This chapter will present my projections of ultimate stationary populations for the eight regional giants and for the LDCs as a group. In this endeavour I am again in good company. Other participants include the World Bank and the United Nations.

I am sure that my colleagues at these institutions would not stake much on their published projections, which run about two centuries into the future in some cases. In deference to them, I should stress that they do not claim more than illustrative status for their projections. I quote from the Technical Notes accompanying the Bank's World Development Indicators (1980):

The estimates of the hypothetical size of the stationary population, the assumed year of reaching replacement-level fertility, and the year of reaching a stationary population are speculative. They should not be regarded as predictions. They are included to provide a summary indication of the long-run implications of recent trends on the basis of highly stylized assumptions. (p. 163.)

I would not ask the reader to place any large bets on my entries, either. As an exercise in good-humoured speculation, however, a comparison of guesses may be instructive. If nothing else, population projections serve to illustrate the unnerving long-run implications of high growth rates. Small gaps between short-run projections have a way of becoming chasms after a century of compounding. And there are chasms indeed between some of my projections and those of the international agencies.

As an introductory exercise, let us consider some competitive projections for the major eight, along with the anticipated dates of arrival at zero population growth. Figure 20 juxtaposes current (1980) population estimates with ultimate population projections from the World Bank and my own simulation runs. My LOW, MEDIUM, and HIGH

FIGURE 20

Projected Ultimate Populations (*)

Country	Current Population (**) (1980)	World Bank (**)	Wheeler		
			Low	Medium	High
Mexico	70	205 (2075)	254 (2100)	317 (2130)	349 (2130)
Brazil	126	345 (2075)	244 (2060)	283 (2075)	319 (2075)
Nigeria	85	425 (2135)	444 (2125)	725 (2160)	944 (2180)
Egypt	42	101 (2105)	74 (2060)	83 (2070)	88 (2070)
Pakistan	82	332 (2150)	467 (2130)	759 (2170)	976 (2190)
India	672	1645 (2150)	1347 (2060)	1499 (2075)	1560 (2080)
Bangladesh	89	314 (2160)	392 (2110)	549 (2145)	649 (2150)
Indonesia	142	350 (2155)	251 (2050)	279 (2070)	294 (2070)
Total	1308	3717	3473	4494	5179

(*) All estimates in millions. Dates for maximum populations are given in parentheses below the estimates.
(**) Source: World Development Indicators: World Development Report (World Bank, 1980)

variants are as described in Chapter 10, except that I have reversed the labels LOW and HIGH to reflect population outcomes.

(i) Stationary populations for the eight giants

If we assume that my LOW and HIGH variants define the bounds for plausible projections for the world defined by my model, it is interesting to note that in no case do the World Bank projections fall within my 'error bounds'.[65] In four cases (Brazil, Egypt, India, Indonesia), the World Bank projection is above my highest figure. In the other four (Mexico, Nigeria, Pakistan, Bangladesh), it is below my lowest. And the numbers involved are obviously not trivial.

How can such large differences be rationalized? One might almost suspect that we were not in the same business. In a sense, of course, that is true: I have already outlined the essential differences in Chapter 9, since the Bank's methodology does not differ much from that of the UN. We are trying to predict the same phenomenon using the same basic set of data, however, and this makes such divergent forecasts rather surprising at first glance.

Some simple data analysis and reflection on the impact of compound growth rates make the results somewhat less surprising. The first major clue lies in the relationship between differences in estimated date of arrival at equilibrium. For each country whose World Bank projection is higher than my highest projection, the Bank's arrival date is also beyond my latest arrival date. For the cases in which the Bank is below my lowest, the arrival dates are scattered but generally earlier than my MEDIUM arrival date (Bangladesh is the exception).

Thus, there is an apparent rough correlation between arrival times and relative stationary populations in the two sets. Now we can turn to a second suggestive pattern: in the Bank projections, the variance in arrival dates within each region is negligible. For Latin America, Brazil and Mexico are both assigned 2075; in South and South-East Asia, Pakistan and India share the year 2150, while Bangladesh and Indonesia are assigned 2155. Egypt and Nigeria are not really in the same region, but they are at least on the African continent and they are assigned dates which are relatively proximate (2105 v. 2135).

Within regions, the variance in my stationary date projections provides a very strong contrast. In my MEDIUM simulation, Brazil is projected to arrive 55 years sooner than Mexico (2075 v. 2130). In Asia, India and Indonesia arrive between 75 and 100 years earlier than Pakistan and Bangladesh (2075 and 2070 v. 2170 and 2145, respectively). The same pattern repeats itself in Africa: Egypt arrives 90 years earlier than Nigeria.

Now a third generalization and we will have enough material to support a discussion on the underlying reasons for the major difference in projections. In Asia, my arrival-date projections and those of the Bank are roughly in agreement for Pakistan and Bangladesh. We differ drastically in the cases of India and Indonesia. In Latin America, we agree exactly for Brazil and disagree substantially about Mexico. In Africa I'm somewhat longer for Nigeria and shorter for Egypt.

Why do I project such different outcomes in the same geographic regions? How can the two sets of projections have roughly similar arrival dates and drastically different stationary population estimates? The answers to these two questions must be found by looking at the two essential demographic numbers: the fertility rate and the mortality rate. As we have seen, there is evidence supporting the notion that the mortality rate has a strong downward trend in most LDCs which are not already in the neighbourhood of the lower limits. Therefore, the main reason for substantial differences in projected arrival dates and stationary populations must lie in differences in the projected time profiles of fertility rate decline.

(ii) Differences in methodology

At this point, it is appropriate to pause for a moment and think about the World Bank's approach to projecting the pattern of fertility decline. Two essential principles govern the projection process. First, it is assumed that a generally observable pattern of decline in fertility will continue world-wide, ultimately affecting countries such as Nigeria and Bangladesh in which there is little evidence of such decline as yet. Second, the socio-economic circumstances which characterize particular countries are taken into account in anticipating the rate at which fertility decline will occur.

The essential horizon for this process is the anticipated year in which the net reproduction rate (NRR) will reach the replacement level of unity (the net reproduction rate is the number of female children which a newborn female can be expected to have in her lifetime, adjusted for her survival probability). The anticipated date and the time path which the NRR will follow as it moves towards unity are the essential parameters in the system. It should be reiterated that they are exogenous in the sense that they arise from the projector's sense of local circumstances but are not affected by any operation of the projection model itself. The final assumption which is crucial to the Bank's projection system has to do with the time profile as women move through the years from fifteen to forty-four.

When these two kinds of assumptions about fertility are combined with pre-imposed age-specific patterns of mortality decline and a known age–sex distribution, it is possible to project a complete demographic future to the point at which the population becomes stable. The two necessary pre-conditions for this result are the assumed stabilization of mortality rates at levels near the currently observable ones in Western countries and the stabilization of the NRR at unity. Once these fundamental parameters are frozen, the population will experience a final period in which the birth-rate exceeds the death-rate because the older generations are outnumbered by the younger groups which are exactly reproducing themselves. Then the population stops growing, having reached its maximum level.

I have no criticism of the World Bank's methodology, since it represents the consistent application of a logical and coherent set of assumptions to the existing data on age distribution for a given population. My own methodology does differ, however, in some crucial respects. First, I have allowed the period fertility rate for all cohorts to shift with changing socio-economic circumstances. In Chapter 5 and Appendix B, I have noted that the international data are consistent with this hypothesis. Secondly, I have moved the locus of assumptions back one step from determination of the time phasing of descent in the NRR to the projected time phasing of the human resource investments which in turn affect the path of fertility decline, among other things. I do think that my approach has one strong advantage: it ties demographic (and economic) variables explicitly to public-policy variables, so that population projections can be tied to anticipated changes in policies concerning health, education, and family planning.

I should point out, however, that my econometric model represents a veritable forest of hypotheses about chains of causation in society. It is consistent with the data, for example, under the assumption that all sample societies are drawn from the same underlying population. There is obviously much glass in my own house here, and I can scarcely throw stones at anyone else's. An additional feature which distinguishes my approach is worth mentioning. There is nothing in my equations which prevents the NRR from declining past unity (just as there is nothing which forces it to reach unity by any particular date). Projected population may therefore peak sooner than would otherwise be the case and then actually decline. In order to compare my numbers with those of the Bank, I have chosen to use the projected maximum values for national populations.

All this said, it is clear that there can be many reasons for divergence between the Bank's projections and my own. In a sense, it is fortunate that the divergence is relatively great in some cases. This difference underlines the degree to which long-run outcomes can vary in response to differing views about the near future. I think that the strategic differences in approach can best be illustrated by looking at some regional pairs.

(iii) The implications

India and Pakistan give us a nice starting-point, because their simulated evolution to the year 2025 has already been discussed in Chapter 10. Recall that India's initial lead in the key variables (schooling, health, family planning) is projected to have a strong impact on relative PQLI status during the next fifty years. When the two trajectories are followed to the point where the birth-rate equals the death-rate, the demographic implication of the divergence is clear. Under MEDIUM assumptions about social policy, India's population reaches its maximum around 2075 at somewhat more than twice its current level. Pakistan reaches the maximum point almost a century later.

The World Bank projection is quite different in both respects. Its stable population for India, while much larger in absolute terms than my MEDIUM projection, is not much larger proportionally. Its date of arrival at stability for India, however, is seventy-five years later than my MEDIUM date. For Pakistan, it projects exactly the same arrival date and a stable population less than half that of my MEDIUM projection.

Since most of my socio-economic data are from the World Bank's own files, we do not differ in our assessment of initial conditions. Pakistan's population growth rate in 1978 was almost 50 per cent higher than India's (3.0 v. 2.1); its estimated total fertility rate was about 34 per cent higher (6.7 v. 5.0); its estimated proportion of women in the reproductive age group (15-44) was slightly lower than India's (40 v. 44). Using these numbers as initial conditions, the Bank projects that Pakistan will arrive at the point where NRR equals unity only fifteen years later than India (2035 v. 2020). From these points, age cohort effects and some presumed differences in mortality rate behaviour determine their arrival at stationary populations in almost the same year.

Two assumptions seem to be implicit in the Bank's projections. The first is that India's current investment in human resources will not yield a continuing pace of fertility decline which matches the experience of countries which are further along the same path. Secondly, there seems to be an implicit assumption that major changes in Pakistan's basic demographic numbers are going to occur in the near future.

The same themes are repeated more moderately in the case of Brazil and Mexico. The Bank's stable population projection for Mexico is lower than my lowest, while its projection exceeds my highest for Brazil. Their time of arrival at NRR = unity is identical in the Bank's projection (2075). I agree exactly (in my MEDIUM projection) about Brazil's arrival date, but differ substantially about Mexico's (2130).

Again, the obvious source of the difference lies in the anticipated profile of fertility decline. Brazil seems ahead at the moment. Its population growth rate and total fertility rate are lower, while its percentage of females in the reproductive years is only slightly higher. On the other hand, Brazil's indices of current efforts for schooling and family planning are somewhat lower. The Bank's projection seems fundamentally based on the assumption that the policies currently in effect in Mexico will drive its birth-rate down faster than the anticipated decline in Brazil. An additional element in the Bank's projection seems to be the observation that Mexico adopted family planning as a national priority in the 1970s while Brazil didn't show much interest. Since family planning is endogenous in my own model, it anticipates rapid increases for both Brazil and Mexico in the 1980s.

Thus, the differences between the projections for Brazil and Mexico can be attributed to reasonable differences in assumptions about the evolution of social policy in the near future. My model seems somewhat more optimistic about Brazil and somewhat more pessimistic about Mexico. As always, the long-run workings of compound growth turn relatively modest differences over the near future into relatively large differences at the horizon.

Basically, the same thing can be said in the Nigerian case. The World Bank's projection for Nigeria is based on the implicit assumption that it will begin a period of rapid fertility decline around 1985. Its anticipated date of arrival at NRR = unity is 2040, twenty years after India and twenty-five years after Brazil and Mexico. The Bank freely admits that this is an arbitrary assumption. In my model, the essential pre-conditions for rapid fertility decline are simply not anticipated to come into being at such short notice. The period of rapid decline is therefore later, and the ultimate population considerably larger. It is worth noting, however, that my LOW projection corresponds almost exactly with the Bank's projection.

A consideration of the other comparative projections would yield essentially the same observations. I might summarize as follows. Where the Bank's projections are substantially lower than those produced by my model, the implicit assumptions must be: (1) that appropriate and massive social policy initiatives will be taken in the next twenty years; and/or (2) that the responsiveness of fertility to changed socio-economic circumstances will be higher in the period 1980–2000 than it was in the period 1960–80. Neither assumption, of course, is falsifiable (or verifiable), given current information. My own projections are based on the assumption that rates of responsiveness in the immediate past (which have been quite substantial) will be about the same in the immediate future.

When the Bank's projections are substantially higher than my own (e.g. Brazil, India, Egypt, Indonesia), I think that there are again two essential reasons for the difference. First, the Bank's staff has applied judgement concerning local circumstances, while my modelling approach excludes this possibility. Thus, for example, my model's optimism about the near future for family planning in Brazil may well not have been replicated in the Bank's considerations. The second basis for the difference may be technical. My model allows the NRR to fall past unity; the Bank's method does not. The implications are obvious.

Ultimately, how should the projections be judged? In fact, they are all simply illustrations. The appeal of my methodology lies mainly in the fact that everything is explicit. Assumptions about human resource policy can be traced right through to demographic outcomes. Much of the same kind of reasoning is undoubtedly present in the Bank's projections, but most of it is implicit. Therefore, although my model is certainly far from a perfect product, I would argue that the approach which it embodies can provide a useful vehicle for discussion. Reasonable people could certainly differ about its responsiveness estimates and their relevance for particular national circumstances. Undeniably, however, the estimated parameters of my model summarize a substantial body of information about behaviour in LDCs during the past twenty years. If other projection approaches involve assumptions which seem either quite optimistic or quite pessimistic by recent international standards, there should be at least some burden on their creators to justify the departure. In this sense, an econometric approach which embeds demographic variables in a structural model can at least play a valuable educational role.

(iv) World population projections

If one summary statement could legitimately be made about the numbers in Figure 20, it would probably be that my projections have higher variance than those of the World Bank. The relative population multiples projected between now and the maximum population point are depicted in descending order in Figure 21.

Obviously, we do not disagree much about the ranking of ultimate effects. In only one case (Nigeria v. Pakistan) do we differ in this regard. It is clear, however, that my high multiples are higher and my lows lower than those of the Bank. The discrepancy in multiples is not too large when my LOW case is used for comparison, but it shows up strongly in the comparison of high multiples in the MEDIUM case.

In both the LOW and MEDIUM cases, my high-end positive discrepancies are larger in magnitude than my low-end negative discrepancies. When total projected populations for all eight countries are considered, this pattern yields the predictable result: the adding of errors leaves the total Bank projection for the eight countries between my LOW and MEDIUM total projections, but toward the LOW end. It is clear that the result is dominated by very large discrepancies for Nigeria, Pakistan, and Bangladesh in the MEDIUM case.

Since this sample is very small (although obviously quite populous) it is of interest to consider the projection of ultimate total LDC population which is implied by the different approaches. In my sample, I have

FIGURE 21
Population Multiples (*)

	World Bank	Wheeler Low	Medium
Nigeria	5.0	5.2	8.5
Pakistan	4.1	5.7	9.3
Bangladesh	3.5	4.4	6.2
Mexico	2.9	3.6	4.5
Brazil	2.7	1.9	2.3
India	2.5	2.0	2.2
Indonesia	2.5	1.8	2.0
Egypt	2.4	1.8	2.0

(*) Defined as (Maximum Population/1980 Population).

thirty-six countries with data sufficient to establish initial conditions for running the model. Figure 22 suggests that this sample is not too bad as a basis for extrapolating to regional cases. For eight Third World subregions, the mean percentage of total countries covered by my sample is 0.35. However, the mean percentage of total subregional population covered is 0.62, and only in the African subregions is the coverage relatively sparse (0.36, 0.55, and 0.40). Thus, I have divided my thirty-six countries by subregion (as indicated in Figure 22); run model simulations under LOW, MEDIUM, and HIGH variants to obtain maximum populations; obtained subregional simulation totals; and then used the sample population percentages as the basis for extrapolating to estimated subregional totals. The results, along with World Bank estimates for the developed countries and China, are presented in Figure 23.

These results essentially replicate the pattern suggested by the eight-nation results (which may not be surprising, since the projected eight-nation totals are over half the projection for all LDCs excluding China). For the full set of LDCs excluding China, the Bank's total comes remarkably close to my LOW projection. My model replicates the Bank's general projection only under quite optimistic assumptions about social policies adopted during the coming two decades. As indicated by the eight-nation results, my simulations (even the LOW ones) generally suggest higher maximum populations than the Bank's for the countries of Central America, Sub-Saharan Africa, and Islamic South Asia. They suggest lower maximum populations for the remaining regions.

Thus, the illustrative projections provided by the World Bank

FIGURE 22
Simulation Sample

Region	POPULATION			COUNTRIES		
	Sample pop. (1980)	Total pop. (1980)	Sample per cent	Sample number	Total number	Sample per cent
Middle America	80.3	121.0	66	5	21	24
South America	168.6	239.0	71	5	12	42
N. Afr. Mid. East	78.2	214.6	36	4	22	18
West Africa	106.6	195.0	55	6	25	24
East, S. Africa	55.1	138.6	40	5	22	23
South-Asia	868.1	883.6	98	4	7	57
South-East Asia	253.3	351.6	72	4	10	40
East Asia	45.4	81.4	56	3	6	50
Total	1655.6	2224.8	(62)	36	125	(35)

FIGURE 23
World Population Projections[a]
(Maximum Population)

Region	1980[b]	World Bank	Wheeler Low[c]	Medium	High
DCs[d]	1078	1313	1307	1307	1307
China	977	1555	1555	1555	1555
LDCs[e]	2332	6903	6784	9067	10622
Total	4387	9771	9646	11929	13484

(a) All numbers in millions.

(b) World Bank estimate (Source: World Bank, World Development Indicators, 1980).

(c) All numbers for the Developed Countries and China are World Bank projections.

(d) Using the Bank's terminology, my Developed Country set includes the Industrialized Countries, the European Centrally-Planned Economies, Yugoslavia, and Israel.

(e) My LDC set includes all Low Income and Middle Income Countries (except Yugoslavia and Israel), the Oil Exporters, and the non-European Centrally-Planned Economies.

suggest a world population of around ten billion at equilibrium. Under the assumption that the historical relationship between GNP and investments in health and education holds, my model projects around twelve billion at the maximum. However, when a more rapid pace of human resource investment is anticipated (as in the case of the World Bank staff), the two projections are quite close. As previously noted, this similar total masks considerable disparity at the regional level.

CHAPTER 12

CONCLUSION

(i) Summary of findings

The simulation results reported in Part IV are based on an econometric analysis of the interactions among human resource policy, economic growth, and demographic change. The construction of a dynamic econometric model has involved much more than parameter estimation, however. Numerous plausible hypotheses concerning the sources of change in LDCs have not received adequate attention in the past, in large part because the relevant data were simply not available.

Two central hypotheses have been tested in this book: the first is that output change and changes in education, health, and nutrition are jointly-determined variables in a simultaneous system. Important predetermined variables in the system include contemporaneous changes in capital, labour, and population; levels of human resource investment in the immediate past; and a set of lagged endogenous variables. Results obtained by three-stage least-squares (3SLS) suggest quite strongly that education and output are jointly determined, and that they may well be joined by nutrition as endogenous variables. The results do not consistently support the hypothesis that health (for which life expectancy is used as a proxy) is a determinant of output.

The second major hypothesis tested in this book is that changes in fertility and family planning activity are jointly determined in a system whose predetermined variables include changes in age cohort representation, per capita income, infant mortality, basic education, and secondary education. The results obtained by 3SLS are quite strong. Several individual results are of particular interest. The impact of family planning on fertility is found to be substantial in the simultaneous model, but not as great as the impact suggested by ordinary least-squares regression.

The results for per capita income and basic education (for which literacy is used as a proxy) are opposed to those generally obtained in cross-section regressions: change in per capita income seems to have a strong effect on fertility, while the measured direct effect of change in basic education appears negligible. Both results should be put in proper perspective. For reasons explained in the text, percentage change in per capita income probably measures changes in the circumstances of poor families with fair accuracy. At the same time, education change seems to have a strong impact on output change, so that schooling does affect fertility, albeit indirectly.

Certain other experiments with the demographic change submodel are also sufficiently noteworthy to be mentioned in this summary. A series of econometric tests on different specifications of the mortality and fertility equations failed to lead to a rejection of the hypothesis that the marginal impacts of predetermined variables are the same for all relevant age cohorts. These results have considerable significance for the demographic submodel. If the hypothesis of equivalent marginal effects cannot be rejected for the death-rate change equation, then predicted death-rate change should serve as a reasonable proxy for change in infant mortality in the fertility equation. The failure to reject the hypothesis of equal marginal effects in the fertility equation itself may have a more important implication: namely, that changes in the socio-economic environment have similar proportional impacts on fertility behaviour for all females of reproductive age. Although it is far from conclusive, this result does suggest that a model which predicts the general fertility rate may do about as well as a more disaggregated, cohort-specific model.

A third noteworthy result has to do with the value of singulate age at marriage (SAM) as an independent predictive variable in a model of fertility-rate determination. As noted in the text, SAM is the only proximate determinant of fertility for which adequate international data have even begun to become available. A series of experiments with a simple structural model yielded the conclusion that SAM does not significantly reduce unexplained variance in a fertility equation when two structural determinants of SAM (education and life expectancy) are also included as reduced-form variables. I should emphasize that this result does not constitute a rejection of the proximate determinants approach, which reflects a very sensible structural model. Rather, it indicates that in a reduced-form predictive fertility equation, measures of changes in education and life expectancy (which are available) can adequately replace a measure of change in SAM (which is not).

The last major result for the demographic submodel pertains to the death-rate equation. In attempting to fit a model of change for the death-rate, I discovered that the most dominant effect is simply 'autonomous change'. While local conditions apparently have some effect on death-rate decline, the main role seems to be played by the generalized diffusion of basic medical technologies such as mass vaccination.

In the course of estimating the full output-change model, I also obtained some interesting subsidiary results. Although my investment equation is undoubtedly the weakest link in the model, some relatively simple econometric work yielded two noteworthy results. The first is that a strong tendency to regress toward the mean is apparent in the international data on investment rates. Countries which enjoyed high rates in 1960 tended, rather strikingly, to experience decreases during the next two decades and conversely. The second finding is that investment rate increase is positively and strongly associated with increase in basic education. It should be noted that the estimated impact of education on investment may be biased upward by the existence of simultaneity over such a long period.

In experiments with the output model, I also obtained some results which have a bearing on the role of extraversion in economic growth. A model in which export growth is a function of relative levels of wages and relevant human resource variables (health and education) fits the data quite well for the 1970s, but not for the 1960s. Export growth itself has almost exactly the same measured impact on output growth in both decades. The inclusion of export growth in the output change equation substantially reduced unexplained variance without having much impact on the measured roles of changes in education and nutrition.

After I tested and estimated a complete model of economic and demographic change, I combined the results with a set of 'housekeeping' equations to form a simulation model. Some results obtained with this model are used in the second half of the book to consider three kinds of questions. First, some experiments with educational policy are used to test for the existence of a 'low-level equilibrium trap' when human resource variables are included as sources of growth. The results seem consistent with the presumed existence of such a trap only when educational progress is entirely suppressed. When typical rates of educational progress are introduced for LDCs, income and other measures of the quality of life (e.g. health, nutrition) move smoothly upward. In an econometric model which is specified to include human resource investments, then, the 'low-level equilibrium trap' doesn't look very threatening.

Since my model does not impose fundamental resource constraints of the type proposed by Enke (1963), the simulation runs do not really constitute a test of the 'high-level equilibrium trap'. It should be noted, however, that the Hazledine–Moreland finding of decreasing returns to scale in a cross-section output equation, which seems to support the Enke hypothesis, may simply reflect specification error. The Hazledine–Moreland work makes no attempt to incorporate any sources of growth other than capital and raw labour input.

The second issue investigated with the simulation model is the cost effectiveness of human resource investment. Varying levels of effort in schooling, medical training, and family planning are introduced in competition with a roughly cost-equivalent autonomous increase in investment to determine whether direct or 'trickle-down' improvement in human resources is the more effective approach. This exercise shows clearly that no general rule is possible in a complex dynamic system when rates of progress in all indices of the physical quality of life (PQLI) are considered. Initial conditions matter. Thus, the simulations yield substantially different results for prototypical African and Latin American cases. The discount rate matters as well, since relative PQLI outcomes change through time in different ways.

For very poor societies (represented by the typical African case), the results suggest that physical investment is the best strategy at the margin only if the discount rate is very high. If the critical horizon is farther removed, education seems to yield better results for all PQLI variables. For very low discount rates, the results suggest that family planning expenditure is superior at the margin. In 'middle income' LDCs as exemplified by the South American case, the apparent superiority of the education option is more pronounced. It supersedes physical investment in all categories almost immediately, and holds its dominant position to the end of the fifty-year simulation period.

In the final simulation exercises, data for various LDCs are introduced as initial conditions for the model and different levels of commitment to human resource investment and family planning activity are used to project alternative futures. Two cases (Kenya v. Tanzania and India v. Pakistan) are used as illustrations of the degree to which presently-observable effort levels are tied to projected outcomes by the model. Sets of demographic projections for eight large LDCs are then produced using three hypothetical levels of social investment effort. My 'medium' projections through the year 2000 (based on average rates of progress in education and medical care during the past two decades) are compared with UN projections completed in 1973. In every case they suggest population growth rates substantially lower than those projected by the UN.

This comparison is admittedly unfair, since my model incorporates data substantially more recent than those available to the UN demographers in the early 1970s. I have attempted to compensate for this by running my simulation variants to the stable population point for the eight LDCs and comparing my projected arrival dates and maximum population levels with the most recent projections of the World Bank. Our projections differ very substantially in all cases, with the World Bank's stable population projections falling below my lowest projections for Mexico, Nigeria, Bangladesh, and Pakistan, and above my highest for Brazil, India, Indonesia, and Egypt. The total population projection for these eight countries by the World Bank is near the lower bound suggested by my simulation (that is, the bound associated with very high rates of progress in schooling, medical care, and family planning).

As a check on this result, I ran the same simulation variations using all thirty-six LDCs for which the necessary data were available and used the results to construct an estimate of the total stable population for LDCs. This result essentially replicates the result for the eight large LDCs. The published World Bank projection of stable population size for all LDCs is very near the projection of my model under the assumption that very substantial human resource and family planning investments will be made in the coming decades. The general pattern of deviation in predictions is the same as that suggested by the eight-nation results: my stable population projections are higher for Central America, Africa, and Islamic South Asia, and lower for South America and South-East Asia.

I would not pretend to claim that my results are 'right' and those of the World Bank 'wrong' in any sense. All such projections are conditional illustrations of possible futures. I would argue, however, that econometrically-based demographic projection is now feasible, and that it might be worth-while for the relevant agencies to consider expanding their efforts to include some structural modelling.

(ii) The limitations of the model

To claim that I have chosen the optimum approach to all questions broached in this book would be presumptuous, to put it mildly. The construction of any edifice, no matter how modest, requires many compromises dictated by the quality of the materials and the nature of the terrain (and, of course, the skill of the architect). I have made many decisions about specification and estimation in the course of this project, for reasons which seem defensible. To aid the reader in drawing independent conclusions, however, I will present a summary critique of my approach.

In the output response equations, the percentage change form indicated by the time derivative of the Cobb–Douglas output equation is allowed to dominate the specification. The form adopted imposes no assumption about returns to scale, but it does impose a factor-neutral specification of the effect of human resource variables on productivity. Unit elasticity of substitution is also inherent in this specification. While a test of the Cobb–Douglas form against an approximate CES specification in time-derivative form did not imply a rejection of the Cobb–Douglas restrictions, I would scarcely call this test conclusive. In any case, degress of freedom were not sufficient to test the constant elasticity form against any linearized variable elasticity specification like the translog.

I certainly think that my specification of the investment function and its relationship to the output model could be improved upon. My equation reflects a simple model of savings behaviour and the assumption that savings are automatically translated into investment. There are clearly limitations here, since many institutional considerations have been ignored. A technical weakness is also evident. Over a seventeen-year period, there is bound to be some simultaneity in the determination of changes in the investment rate and changes in output. The problem for estimation is the second order nature of this relationship between the two variables. Changes in output and other variables lead to a change in the investment rate, but it is the new level of the investment rate which determines changes in the capital stock and subsequently in output. A model of this second order relationship could have been estimated, but the whole exercise simply seemed too unwieldly to me. Implicitly, I am betting that the simultaneity biases in my estimates of the dynamic relations between output and capital are not severe.

My demographic submodel also has evident weaknesses. My specification of functional forms is not exactly *ad hoc*, but it is not exactly rigorous, either. Since I know of no other work on time-change estimation of fertility functions, I have had no prior work to guide me. Certain specifications, as I noted, have been suggested by theory: linear additivity in changes for age cohort percentages, and percentage change in per capita income, for example. The specification of the contribution of mortality change to fertility decline is non-linear, and simply reflects my own inspection of the evident bivariate relationship between the two variables. In the death-rate equation, the final form is the result of a substantial amount of experimentation. Ironically, the primary result of this experimentation is the conclusion that the driving force behind death-rate decline is largely autonomous.

Many of the simulation equations are tied to the economic and demographic regression models, and they reflect the associated strengths and weaknesses. A word is in order, however, about some of the housekeeping equations. My data set does not include country-specific observations on fertility and mortality by age cohort. In many cases, as I have noted, such data simply do not exist. I have therefore had to run the simulation model using general fertility and death-rates. The death-rate is applied as a probability which is age–sex independent. This is necessary for consistency with the aggregate baseline data, even though the predicted rate itself is sensitive to changes in age cohorts. Over a lifetime, of course, the errors associated with this process 'average out' to a great degree (that is, the general rate will tend to underestimate risk for the young and old, while overestimating it in the middle). I would have much preferred to work with age–sex specific rates for particular countries, however.

The same sort of thing can be said about fertility rates: I have had to apply the same general fertility rate to all surviving females of reproductive age. The result should be an overestimate of fertility in the earliest and latest years and an underestimate for the prime years. Again, the errors should roughly balance, so that the implicit net reproduction rate for each cohort should be about right, but I would have preferred to use age-specific fertility rates as baseline data for the simulations. I know that estimates of relative rates are available for some countries, and at least at the level of regional approximation for others. In an attempt at purity which is perhaps misguided, I have refrained from using any such regional approximations. They could easily be introduced into the model, however.

I will now turn briefly to the simulation exercises themselves. It is perfectly reasonable to criticize my choice of exogenous variable paths for the countries whose socio-economic futures are projected. I have varied my growth rates of schooling and medical care around the means prevailing among LDCs during the past two decades. It could be argued that I should have based my projections for particular countries on their own past growth rates or regional growth rates. There are arguments for and against these options which mirror the debate about whether a country's long-run future is better predicted with a national model fitted to time series data or a model fitted to an international cross-section of changes.

I have chosen the international variant, and this may be one reason why my individual country projections differ so substantially from those of the World Bank. I have not run the simulations using national change rates as the bases for extrapolation, but it would probably be educational to do so. The non-econometric parts of the simulation model can be changed at will, as long as internal consistency is preserved. I would therefore regard a criticism of the extrapolation base as a difference over detail rather than substance. It is undoubtedly true, however, that changing bases would lead to very different long-run projections in some cases.

(iii) Postlude

I would like to continue a venerable tradition by closing this book on a note of hope and a note of caution. First, the caution: how believable are the econometric results which I have reported? Let me wend my way toward my autocritique with a brief historical digression. In the days when matrices were inverted by hand, economics and statistics coexisted rather comfortably. It was simply too much trouble to do many econometric 'experiments', so the classical canons of hypothesis-testing were (however grudgingly) respected. Enter the digital computer. After twenty years of 'technical progress', the paths of academe are being worn smooth by graduate assistants groaning under the weight of yard-thick printouts. Behind closed doors, there is often considerable browsing before 'hypotheses' are born. We certainly have no paucity of results these days. As to whether we know more than Schumpeter, or Keynes, or Marx . . . I will leave such questions to the mature reflection of the reader and move on to my auto-critique.

I too have perused my share of printouts. In a personal attempt to 'come clean' on this score, I have included a chronicle of unsuccessful experiments in each econometric chapter. For those variables which survived the experiments, I generally chose the specification which seemed to fit the data best. My results are considerably more than lucky shots. As I have noted, however, most of the 'significant' variables remain significant no matter what specification is employed.

Having said this, I must immediately add that the standard errors reported with the final estimates in this book have little of Divine Truth about them. I feel relatively good about the general magnitudes of the parameter estimates and the associated point predictions in the simulations, but I do not think that formal confidence interval construction for the predictions is warranted.

To the question 'How believable?' then, I must respond with what I hope are artful gestures and a shrug. The model and its predictions reflect the virtues of believable specification, internal consistency, and empirical grounding. If this kind of modelling approach continues to hold up as more and better data become available, then I'll cheerfully become more assertive in its defence. Undoubtedly, some variables which have looked significant in subsamples drawn from the past two decades will join the casualty list as the years go by.

Having completed my expiatory ritual, I would like to close on a more positive note. I can honestly report that the simulations themselves have not been subjected to tinkering—I was stuck with my parameter estimates. And the model does yield wonderfully stable and plausible paths for the endogenous variables, even many decades into the future. It digests a considerable amount of information about a society—over thirty variable values—before spinning its predictive web.

Although this richness of empirical detail is obviously attractive, it does create presentational problems. Any change in an initial condition or an exogenous variable path causes a different set of outcomes to be projected for a particular country. At my command, the computer could generate an encyclopaedia at reasonable cost. This does not seem necessary. In a real sense, the model itself is the simulation. For this reason, I have devoted much of the book to econometric analysis. The exercises in Part IV are illustrations of the model's operation which give a sense of the importance of human resource policy in promoting economic and demographic change. Many other experiments could obviously have been performed.

Where should we go from here? In the final analysis, a decision to go further with this kind of work has to be based on the conviction that we can learn something of value. Certainly, there are many social scientists who have become sceptical about the utility of more exercises in statistical fitting on international data. Economists have shown a particular tendency to 'burrow in' in recent years, and the prestige of micro-econometrics is unquestionably ascendant. But it seems to me that we would be unwise to cede the quantitative discussion of global futures to the authors of such pearls as *The Population Bomb* and *The Limits to Growth*. Things are indeed 'more complicated than that'. If policy makers in poor countries are interested in drawing on the existing fund of world experience, there is no reason why econometrics should not be pressed into service to aid them.

APPENDICES

A. LITERACY AND PRODUCTIVITY:
A TWO-EQUATION MODEL

The response equations estimated for this book have all incorporated the change in calories consumed as a complement to literacy change in the determination of intraperiod output change. As noted in Chapter 3, the nutrition results are rendered ambiguous by the possibility that they measure the efficiency impact of differential agricultural growth as well as the impact of nutritional improvement.

One possible response to this ambiguity could be an arbitrary rejection of the calorie consumption measure as a valid component of the output equation. If nutrition were excluded, the resulting growth model would identify basic education as the only contributor to productivity growth. In Figure 24 results for an education-augmenting growth model are presented. Although only the output equation results are presented, all three-stage estimates have been produced in association with a literacy change equation identical to the one employed previously.

It is clear that the exclusion of nutrition change from the output equation has no real consequence for the remaining estimates. Again, the estimated effect of literacy change in the output equation exhibits an apparent decline between the first and second decades. Although the 95 per cent confidence intervals for the two estimates overlap slightly, it may well be that the impact of reported literacy change has declined.

It is not clear, of course, that the true impact of literacy has declined. During the decade of the seventies, a general enthusiasm for rapid human-resource development may have have led to widespread optimism in national self-evaluation of educational performance. As previously mentioned, Tanzania and Somalia have been excluded from all estimates because the reported impacts of their adult literacy campaigns seem neither plausible nor appropriate as measures of the kind of educational achievement which is of interest here. In any case, the results in all three sets of estimates are again consistent with the hypothesis that basic education has a significant impact on productivity.

FIGURE 24
Literacy and Productivity Change: A Two-equation Model (*)

1960–1970(**)

OBS

$$\langle dq \rangle = .0147 + .161\star\langle dk \rangle + .222\star\langle dl \rangle + .0254\star[E\{t\} - E\{t-1\}]$$
$$\quad\ (.1278)\ (.030) \qquad (.341) \qquad (.0055)$$

40

1970–1977

$$\langle dq \rangle = -.0855 + .187\star\langle dk \rangle + .498\star\langle dl \rangle + .0080\star[E\{t\} - E\{t-1\}]$$
$$\quad\ (.0798)\ (.037) \qquad (.342) \qquad (.0041)$$

44

Pooled Data

$$\langle dq \rangle = [.006 - .069\star D70] + .168\star\langle dk \rangle + .346\star\langle dl \rangle$$
$$\quad\ (.087)\ (.044) \qquad\quad (.022) \qquad (.237)$$

$$\quad\ + .018\star[E\{t\} - E\{t-1\}]$$
$$\quad\ (.0041)$$

84

(*) Standard errors in parentheses beneath coefficients.
(**) Each of the three equations presented below has been estimated by three-stage least-squares along with the literacy change equation whose specification has been seen several times. Since the results for the second equations are essentially identical with those for previous models, they have not been included here.

B. AGE COHORTS IN DEMOGRAPHIC
CHANGE EQUATIONS

In the discussion of fertility and death-rate determination which absorbed Part II of this book, a relatively simple model of age-cohort impact was specified and estimated. Although mention was made of more intricate models, a full discussion was deferred to this Appendix in the interests of readability.

At first, it may seem illusory to suppose that the differential impacts of causal variables across age cohorts can be estimated without cohort-specific data. While it is true that the absence of such data prevents the specification and estimation of completely general models, it is certainly possible to use the available numbers to good effect. The key to this possibility lies in the fact that the general fertility rate and the crude death-rate are weighted averages of age-specific rates. A brief mathematical development can be used to show that cohort-specific sensitivities can be measured once a model of responsiveness has been imposed. Although either accumulation parameter could be employed for the demonstration, the fertility rate will be used here.

We will define the general fertility rate as:

(12) $F = (W1/W) \star f1 + (W2/W) \star f2 + \ldots + (Wn/W) \star fn$

where
F = General fertility rate
Wk = Number of women in reproductive age cohort k
W = Total women of child-bearing age
fk = Fertility rate of women in age cohort k

We are in possession of crude birth-rates from World Bank data and age cohort estimates from United Nations data, but we lack cohort-specific fertility rates. This sort of problem is not uncommon in econometrics. The standard response is to replace the unknown with its known determinants in a mathematically-specified relationship whose parameters can be estimated.

In order to develop some plausible fertility determination models, we will suppose initially that fertility in each age cohort responds to one variable, X. In addition, we will lend flexibility to the model by supposing that the marginal effect of X differs across cohorts. Thus, for the kth cohort, we would have a simple linear model of fertility determination:

(13) $fk = ak1 + ak2 \star X + uk$

where uk is a random, additive error term and the ak's are parameters

If we substitute into the expression for the general fertility rate, we obtain:

$$(14) \quad F = (W1/W)\star[a11 + a12\star X + u1] + (W2/W)\star[a21 + a22\star X + u2]$$
$$+ \ldots + (Wn/W)\star[an1 + an2\star X + un]$$
$$= a11\star(W1/W) + a12\star(W1/W)\star X + a21\star(W2/W)$$
$$+ a22\star(W2/W)\star X + \ldots + an1\star(Wn/W) + an2\star(Wn/W)\star X$$
$$+ [u1\star(W1/W) + \ldots + un\star(Wn/W)].$$

Since it is clear that $W = W1 + \ldots + Wn$, the above reduces to:

$$(15) \quad F = (a11 - an1)\star(W1/W) + (a12 - an2)\star(W1/W)\star X$$
$$+ (a21 - an1)\star(W2/W) + (a22 - an2)\star(W2/W)\star X + \ldots$$
$$+ an1 + an2\star X + e$$

where $e =$ the additive sum of weighted error terms previously specified

An unconstrained linear model which allows X to have a differential impact across age cohorts will be specified as (15) above. This model can usefully be contrasted with a simpler version, which constrains all marginal impacts of X to be equal:

$$(16a) \quad a12 = a22 = \ldots = an2$$

All difference coefficients of X-terms in the former equation become zero in this constrained specification, and we have:

$$(16b) \quad F = (a11 - an1)\star(W1/W) + (a21 - an1)\star(W2/W) + \ldots$$
$$+ an1 + an2\star X + e$$

The constrained and unconstrained versions of the linear model can be compared statistically. With multiple age cohorts and several causal variables, it is clear that the number of right-hand terms in the unconstrained version of this model is likely to be burdensome. A statistical test on the multiple coefficient constraints implied by the simple version of the model is therefore appealing. If the simple linear model cannot be rejected statistically, we are bound to gain precision in estimation by adopting it.

The two models of cohort-specific determination proposed thus far incorporate assumptions about responsiveness which are at opposite extremes. In the unconstrained version, estimated marginal impacts are left completely free to vary as the data dictate. In the constrained version, they are all forced to equality. It is also possible to specify an intermediate alternative which accords some flexibility to coefficient estimates without sacrificing degrees of freedom. Instead of constraining all marginal coefficients to be equal, this intermediate form imposes a constant multiplicative relationship across cohorts. Thus:

(17) $F = (W1/W) \star f1 + (W2/W) \star f2 + \ldots + (Wn/W) \star fn$

$= (W1/W) \star f1 + (W2/W) \star c2 \star f1 + \ldots + (Wn/W) \star cn \star f1$

where the c's are taken to be unvarying multiplicative constants

With age cohort relationships specified in stochastic form as before (and noting that the female age cohort ratios sum to 1), we have:

(18) $F = (W1/W) \star [a11 + a12 \star X] + \ldots + (Wn/W) \star cn \star [a11 + a12 \star X]$

$+ e = [cn + (1 - cn) \star (W1/W) + (c2 - cn) \star (W2/W) + \ldots]$

$\star [a11 + a12 \star X] + e$

This intermediate model is nonlinear in the parameters, but it can be estimated using maximum likelihood methods.

Some comparative estimates

The discussion in the first part of this Appendix was focused on the problem of estimating differential marginal impacts across age cohort groups for fertility rates. It is clear that exactly the same reasoning could be applied to the design of cohort-sensitive death-rate models. In this section, the models developed previously will be compared statistically for fertility rates and death-rates, using cross-section data for 1977. In each case, the variables employed are those which are already familiar from the difference equations presented in Part II.

Fertility estimates

In the fertility equations, the general fertility rate (F) across countries is related to data on family planning activity (PL), the crude death-rate (D), per capita income (Q/P), and three age cohorts for childbearing females (W1524, W2534, W3549). Since the three age cohort percentages sum to one, W3549 has been selected as the residual percentage.

All three models developed in the previous section have been estimated using the same data. The results are presented in Figure 25.

The results in Figure 25 indicate that the more complex models do not make a significant marginal contribution to the explanation of fertility rate differentials. The unconstrained linear model is obviously plagued by multicollinearity, and individual estimates seem to wander randomly. An application of the standard F-test yields the conclusion that the full set of constraints implied by the hypothesis of equal marginal impacts cannot be rejected. (The small increase in the sum of squared residuals makes this an obvious result.) At the same time, all available measures of goodness of fit ($R \star \star 2$, SSR) suggest that the constrained linear model fits better than its nonlinear counterpart.

FIGURE 25
Comparative Results—Fertility Equations (*)

LINEAR UNCONSTRAINED MODEL

$F = -942.688 - 8.2886 \star PL - 4.9425 \star D + 2.2174 \star D \star\star 2 + .83249 \star (Q/P)$
    (1833.27) (25.0729)   (221.7)   (7.20)   (.8099)

    $+ 2192.44 \star W1524 + 8.9219 \star PL \star W1524 - 57.985 \star D \star W1524$
    (2397.65)   (32.62)   (270.2)

    $- .3824 \star D \star\star 2 \star W1524 - 1.5604 \star (Q/P) \star W1524 + 227.466 \star W2534$
    (8.34)   (1.369)   (4060.1)

    $+ 9.6382 \star PL \star W2534 + 159.22 \star D \star W2534 - 8.501 \star D \star\star 2 \star W2534$
    (55.18)   (497.8)   (16.40)

    $- .6227 \star (Q/P) \star W2534$
    (1.162)

OBS = 65   R$\star\star$2 = .85   SSR = 13613.2   F(14/50) = 26.1

LINEAR CONSTRAINED MODEL

$F = -560.866 + 982.780 \star W1524 + 706.839 \star W2534 - 1.7762 \star PL$
    (108.718) (131.328)   (217.582)   (.4713)

    $+ 15.9139 \star D - .3897 \star D \star\star 2 - .01402 \star (Q/P)$
    (3.017)   (.0919)   (.0114)

OBS = 65   R$\star\star$2 = .86   SSR = 14431.7   F(6/58) = 66.1

NONLINEAR MODEL

$F = [-1.520 + 3.555 \star W1524 + 2.576 \star W2534]$
    (.597) (1.212)   (1.212)

    $\star [98.312 - 2.4192 \star PL + 19.963 \star D - .4824 \star D \star\star 2 - .0216 \star (Q/P)]$
    (.7322) (.6268)   (10.418)   (.2723)   (.0134)

OBS = 65   R$\star\star$2 = .84   SSR = 15857.8

(*) Standard errors in parentheses beneath coefficients.

Certainly, the experiments undertaken here do not exhaust the econometric possibilities which could be considered if actual cohort-specific fertility data were available. In the absence of such data, it has still been possible to compare three different models of responsiveness. The statistical evidence points toward the provisional acceptance of the simplest model, which imposes equal marginal impacts of causal variables on cohort-specific fertility rates. It should be noted that the results still suggest constant cohort-specific differences.

FIGURE 26
Comparative Results—Death-rate Equations (*)

LINEAR UNCONSTRAINED MODEL

$$D = -16.692 + 6.782E - 4 \star M + 53.512 \star Y - 7.99E - 4 \star Y \star M + 46.725 \star O$$
$$\quad\ (14.159)\quad (.0015)\qquad\ (24.84)\qquad\ (.0027)\qquad\quad (32.85)$$

$$\quad -.0010 \star O \star M$$
$$\quad\ (.0029)$$

OBS = 68   R★★2 = .56   SSR = 805.8   F(5/62) = 18.0

LINEAR CONSTRAINED MODEL

$$D = -14.085 + 2.203E - 4 \star M + 49.009 \star Y + 40.624 \star O$$
$$\quad\ (11.736)\ (2.670 \star E - 5)\quad (20.583)\quad (27.240)$$

OBS = 68   R★★2 = .57   SSR = 807.4   F(3/64) = 30.8

NONLINEAR MODEL

$$D = [-1.0184 + 3.9832 \star Y + 3.1664 \star O] \star [10.9809 + .00021 \star M]$$
$$\quad\ (.8174)\ (1.244)\qquad (1.803)\qquad\quad (1.085)\ (3.72E - 5)$$

OBS = 68   R★★2 = .56   SSR = 810.7

(*) Standard errors in parentheses beneath coefficients.

Death-rate estimates

The crude death-rate and the general fertility rate for a population are similar in the sense that both are weighted averages of cohort-specific rates. Thus, the theoretical development of three comparative models of fertility rate determination can be essentially replicated in the case of the death-rate. Again, cross-section data for 1977 have been employed in the comparative analysis. The regression equations have been fitted using the variables which proved to have a significant association with death-rate changes in a cross-section of time differences. The results are presented in Figure 26.

Once again, the evidence suggests provisional acceptance of the constrained linear model. The F-test on the multiple coefficient constraints fails resoundingly to reject the hypothesis of equal marginal impacts. At the same time, the nonlinear fixed-ratio alternative seems inferior by the standard measures of goodness-of-fit. On the basis of the evidence currently available, it seems appropriate to conclude that cohort-specific death rates across countries differ significantly only by a constant term. The hypothesis that medical personnel affect all cohorts equally at the margin certainly cannot be rejected at any reasonable level of statistical confidence.

C. SAMPLE COUNTRIES

In Chapter 2, considerable attention was paid to the problem of data scarcity when time-change equations are estimated in this context. Each intersection of variables contains a different subset of observations from the full group of eighty-eight countries. Under such circumstances, it is unwise to ignore the risk that a particular intersection sample may be entirely unrepresentative of the full set. In this Appendix the intersection samples for the principal output and demographic models are listed. It might have been supposed *a priori* that data availability was positively associated with per capita income. Fortunately, this does not seem to have been the case. The smaller samples bear a surprising resemblance to random draws, with no detectable bias in favour of a particular region or income level.

FIGURE 27

Sample Countries—Closed Economy

1960s	1970s
Portugal	Portugal
Greece	Turkey
Spain	Yugoslavia
Turkey	Morocco
Yugoslavia	Tunisia
Morocco	Chad
Tunisia	Ethiopia
Cameroon	Ghana
Zaire	Ivory Coast
Ghana	Kenya
Ivory Coast	Madagascar
Kenya	Malawi
Liberia	Mauritania
Senegal	Senegal
Somalia	Sierra Leone
Sudan	Sudan
Tanzania	Togo
Togo	Upper Volta
Dominican Republic	Zambia
El Salvador	Dominican Republic
Jamaica	El Salvador
Mexico	Jamaica
Panama	Mexico
Argentina	Nicaragua
Bolivia	Panama
Brazil	Argentina
Chile	Bolivia
Colombia	Brazil
Paraguay	Chile
Syria	Colombia
Afghanistan	Paraguay
Sri Lanka	Uruguay
India	Syria
Pakistan	Afghanistan
Hong Kong	Sri Lanka
South Korea	India
Malaysia	Pakistan
Philippines	Hong Kong
Thailand	South Korea
	Malaysia
	Philippines
	Singapore
	Thailand

FIGURE 28
Sample Countries—Life Expectancy Equation

Portugal	Bolivia
Greece	Brazil
Spain	Chile
Turkey	Colombia
Yugoslavia	Paraguay
Morocco	Uruguay
Tunisia	Israel
Cameroon	Syria
Chad	Afghanistan
Zaire	India
Ethiopia	Nepal
Ghana	Pakistan
Guinea	Hong Kong
Ivory Coast	South Korea
Kenya	Malaysia
Liberia	Singapore
Madagascar	Thailand
Malawi	
Mauritania	
Senegal	
Sierra Leone	
Somalia	
Sudan	
Tanzania	
Togo	
Upper Volta	
Zambia	
Dominican Republic	
El Salvador	
Haiti	
Jamaica	
Mexico	
Nicaragua	
Panama	
Argentina	

FIGURE 29
Sample Countries—Full Investment Equation

Turkey
Yugoslavia
Morocco
Tunisia
Egypt
Burundi
Benin
Ghana
Ivory Coast
Kenya
Rwanda
Senegal
Togo
Dominican Republic
El Salvador
Guatemala
Honduras
Jamaica
Mexico
Panama

Bolivia
Brazil
Chile
Colombia
Paraguay
Peru
Afghanistan
Burma
Sri Lanka
India
Pakistan
Bangladesh
Taiwan
Hong Kong
South Korea
Malaysia
Philippines
Thailand
Papua New Guinea

FIGURE 30
Sample Countries—Fertility Change Model

Turkey	Dominican Republic
Morocco	El Salvador
Tunisia	Guatemala
Egypt	Haiti
Cameroon	Honduras
Central Afr. Rep.	Jamaica
Zaire	Mexico
Ethiopia	Nicaragua
Ghana	Panama
Guinea	Bolivia
Ivory Coast	Brazil
Kenya	Chile
Lesotho	Colombia
Liberia	Paraguay
Madagascar	Peru
Malawi	Jordan
Mali	Lebanon
Mauritania	Syria
Niger	Afghanistan
Rwanda	Burma
Senegal	Sri Lanka
Sierra Leone	India
Somalia	Nepal
Sudan	Pakistan
Tanzania	Bangladesh
Togo	Hong Kong
Uganda	South Korea
Upper Volta	Laos
Zambia	Malaysia
Costa Rica	Philippines
	Singapore
	Thailand

FIGURE 31
Sample Countries—Death-rate Equation

Portugal	Upper Volta
Greece	Zambia
Spain	Costa Rica
Turkey	El Salvador
Yugoslavia	Guatemala
Morocco	Haiti
Tunisia	Jamaica
Egypt	Mexico
Burundi	Nicaragua
Cameroon	Panama
Central Afr. Rep.	Argentina
Chad	Bolivia
Zaire	Brazil
Benin	Chile
Ethiopia	Colombia
Ghana	Paraguay
Guinea	Peru
Ivory Coast	Uruguay
Kenya	Jordan
Liberia	Syria
Madagascar	Afghanistan
Malawi	Burma
Mali	Sri Lanka
Mauritania	India
Niger	Nepal
Rwanda	Pakistan
Senegal	Hong Kong
Sierra Leone	South Korea
Somalia	Laos
Sudan	Malaysia
Tanzania	Singapore
Togo	Thailand
	Papua New Guinea

D. REVISED SIMULATION MODEL EQUATIONS

(1) Low $S =$ IF $S(-1) \star 1.04$ LT 140 THEN $S(-1) \star 1.04$
ELSE 140

     Medium $S =$ IF $S(-1) \star 1.08$ LT 140 THEN $S(-1) \star 1.08$
ELSE 140

     High $S =$ IF $S(-1) \star 1.16$ LT 140 THEN $S(-1) \star 1.16$
ELSE 140

(2) Low $M = M(-1) \star\star .99$
    Medium $M = M(-1) \star\star .9775$
    High $M = M(-1) \star\star .95$

(3) $SEC =$ IF $SEC(-1)$ LE 60 THEN $1.48243 \star (SEC(-1))$
    $- .000123 \star SEC(-1) \star\star 3$ ELSE $SEC(-1) + 2$

(4) $PM1 = 1 - D(-1)/1000$

(5) $PM2 = (1 - D(-1)/1000) \star\star 7$

(6) $P17 = P(-1) \star B(-1)/1000 \star (1 + PM1 + PM1 \star\star 2 + PM1 \star\star 3$
    $+ PM1 \star\star 4 + PM1 \star\star 5 + PM1 \star\star 6)$

(7) $P814 = P17(-1) \star PM2$

(8) $Y = P17 + P814$

(9) $A = (A(-1) + P814(-1)) \star PM2$

(10) $P = Y + A$

(11) $PY = Y/P$

(12) $W1519 = 5/7 \star .5 \star P814(-1) \star PM2$

(13) $W2024 = W1519(-1) \star PM2$

(14) $W2529 = W2024(-1) \star PM2$

(15) $W3034 = W2529(-1) \star PM2$

(16) $W3539 = W3034(-1){\star}PM2$

(17) $W4044 = W3539(-1){\star}PM2$

(18) $W4549 = W4044(-1){\star}PM2$

(19) $W2534 = W2529 + W3034$

(20) $W1549 = W1519 + W2024 + W2529 + W3034 + W3539$
$+ W4044 + W4549$

(21) $PW2435 = W2534/W1549$

(22) $PO = 1 - PY - 2{\star}W1549/P$

(23) $DP = (P - P(-1))/P(-1)$

(24) $DA = (A - A(-1))/A(-1)$

(25) $DL = DA$

(26) $DK = 7{\star}I(-1)/100$

(27) $DQ = .012 + .146{\star}DK + .565{\star}DL + 1.011{\star}DN$
$+ .0096{\star}(E - E(-1))$

(28) $DN = -.04 + (3.259 - .674{\star}\text{LOG}(N(-1))){\star}(DQ - DP)$
$+ .042{\star}\text{LOG}((Q/P)(-1)/N(-1))$

(29) $E = E(-1){\star}(1/(1 + DA)) - .996 + .755{\star}(S(-1)$
$+ S(-2))/2{\star}(DA/(1 + DA)) + 12.291{\star}(DQ - DP)$

(30) $DH = -.124 + 6.948{\star}1/H(-1) + .142{\star}DH(-1)$
$+ (.573 - .144{\star}\text{LOG}(H(-1))){\star}(DQ - DP)$
$+ .077{\star}DN(-1) + .027{\star}E(-1)/H(-1)$
$+ 1.10E - 5{\star}M(-1)/H(-1)$
$+ .01{\star}S(-1)/H(-1)$

(31) $Q/P = Q/P(-1){\star}(1 + DQ - DP)$

(32) $H = H(-1){\star}(1 + DH)$

(33)   Low/Medium $I = 8.34446 + .30611 \star I(-2)$
$$+ 5.30167 \star ((Q/P) - (Q/P)(-2))/(Q/P)(-2)$$
$$+ 3.07052 \star (E - E(-2))/I(-2)$$
$$+ 2.18293 \star (H - H(-2))/I(-2)$$
   High $I = 3 + 8.3446 + .30611 \star I(-2) + 5.30167 \star ((Q/P)$
$$- (Q/P)(-2))/(Q/P)(-2)$$
$$+ 3.07052 \star (E - E(-2))/I(-2)$$
$$+ 2.18293 \star (H - H(-2))/I(-2)$$

(34) $N = N(-1) \star (1 + DN)$

(35) $D = 6.6523 - .0671 \star D(-2) + .0193 \star D(-2) \star\star 2$
$$+ 2.4956E - 5 \star M(-2) + 19.3986 \star (PY - PY(-2))$$
$$+ 19.8577 \star (PO - PO(-2))$$

(36) $BC = .15902 \star SEC(-1) - 27.1634 \star (PW2534 - PW2534(-1))$
$$- 1.3972 \star (D - D(-1)) + .03582 \star (D \star\star 2 - D(-1) \star\star 2)$$
$$+ 2.23525 \star ((Q/P) - (Q/P)(-1))/(Q/P)(-1)$$

(37)   Low $PLAN =$ IF $.5 \star BC + PPLAN(-1)$ LT 30 THEN
$$.5 \star BC \text{ ELSE } 30 - PPLAN(-1)$$
   Medium $PLAN =$ IF $BC + PPLAN(-1)$ LT 30 THEN
$$BC \text{ ELSE } 30 - PPLAN(-1)$$
   High $PLAN =$ IF $BC + 10 + PPLAN(-1)$ LT 30 THEN
$$BC + 10 \text{ ELSE } 30 - PPLAN(-1)$$

(38) $PPLAN = PPLAN(-1) + PLAN$

(39) $DFR = 187.338 \star (PW2534 - PW2534(-1)) +$
$$+ 9.63614 \star (D - D(-1)) - .2470 \star (D \star\star 2 - D(-1) \star\star 2)$$
$$- 15.4159 \star [Q/P - Q/P(-1)]/Q/P(-1)$$
$$- 1.3122 \star PLAN$$

(40) $FR =$ IF $FR(-1) + DFR$ GE 40 THEN $FR(-1)$ ELSE 40

(41) $PF = W1549/P$

(42) $B = FR \star PF$

NOTES

1. It is wrong to claim that all economists have viewed population growth as a problem. Simon (1977) has recently emerged as a strong advocate of the position that moderate population growth can promote economic development. In this connection, Simon has produced his own genealogy. It includes (inevitably) Keynes (1937), von Thunen (1966), and Kuznets (1973). Although my work was not intended as a contribution to the debate between pro- and anti-natalists, my econometric results are obviously relevant. This subject is explored in the final part of the book.

2. As both Perlman (1975) and Simon (1977) have noted, Malthus's memory is unjustly sullied by this label. In the later editions of his *Essay*, Malthus concluded that technological progress could outrun population growth because the latter could be checked by 'moral restraint'.

3. Econometric work on factor-augmentation in industrial societies has generally used time series to measure the contribution of education (see Intriligator (1965), Denison (1967), and Barger (1969)). Econometric work on the sources of growth in LDCs has tended to compensate for data scarcity by adopting a cross-sectional approach (Robinson (1971)). Fallon and Layard (1975) have estimated the degree of complementarity between skills and physical capital in productivity determination across countries. Other recent papers (Correa (1970), Hicks (1979), Wheeler (1980)) have attempted to extend the study of sources of growth in LDCs to include health and nutrition, as well as education.

4. The debate concerning social returns to education has been long and heated. Fields (1980) notes that most work suffers from a failure to take simultaneity into account in analysing the intertemporal association between change in income and change in education. Among those who have done empirical work on the relationship between education and productivity change, conclusions are very mixed. A study of agricultural productivity by Hayami and Ruttan (1970) suggests an important role for technical and general education in explaining the differential between rich and poor countries. This conclusion is supported by the extensive comparative work of Psacharopoulos (1973), who has calculated a substantial average social rate of return across countries. Among the sceptics, contrary evidence is cited by Nadiri (1972), who concludes from a survey of the literature that education has generally been unimportant as a determinant of differentials across countries, although within-country contributions often appear significant. Blaug (1973, 1978) and others have explained this seeming paradox with a 'credentialist' interpretation of within-country differentials.

Micro-level studies seem to have been no more successful in resolving this controversy than their macro-level counterparts. In an excellent study of labour absorption in the Japanese cotton-spinning industry, Saxonhouse (1977) finds very strong evidence to support the hypothesis of complementarity between capital and educated labour. On the other hand, some direct studies of the relationship between education and the industrial performance of workers have failed to discern any such association (see, for example, Fuller (1975)).

5. A few micro-level studies of the relationship between nutrition and productivity have been attempted. See Basta and Churchill (1974).

6. Support for this hypothesis has been found by Koh (1977) in the case of entrepreneurial behaviour in Japan.

7. See Chapter 4 for a detailed discussion of the fertility debate. For good recent surveys, see Leibenstein (1974) and Birdsall (1980).

8. There is, of course, nothing in the economic theory of fertility which guarantees the dominance of the opportunity cost effect. The consensus reflects a strong negative association between per capita income and fertility which is often evident in cross-section regressions. As Simon (1974, 1977) has noted, short-run time series analyses tend to show a positive relationship between income and fertility because it takes time for the income-induced changes in family life to have an impact on the evaluation of opportunity costs. Dyson *et al.* (1978) have recently published work on the long-run dynamic links joining fertility, mortality, and income.

9. Existing cross-sectional evidence concerning the relationship between education and fertility has been summarized in Cochrane (1979). In international cross-section regressions, the literacy rate has exhibited one of the strongest negative associations with fertility.

10. Actually, things may be more complicated than this. As Birdsall (1980) notes, high infant mortality can contribute to high fertility for a biological reason: lactation delays the return of regular ovulation, so that the survival of infants produces a natural contraceptive effect over prolonged periods. Scrimshaw (1978) has raised the possibility that infant mortality and fertility are simultaneously determined. High fertility in poor environments can lead to more infant deaths per family, for example.

11. This index was first proposed by Robert Lapham and Parker Mauldin. I will refer to it as the Mauldin–Berelson index because of its association with their work (1978) which is cited in this study.

12. This is not to say, of course, that health has no effect on productivity in poor countries. The results simply suggest that the available measure is not very helpful in gauging the marginal effect of health improvements at the macro level.

13. Recent work by Morawetz (1977) illustrates this phenomenon. Morawetz presents results for a large number of regressions relating indices of basic needs fulfilment to levels of per capita GNP. For 30 of 32 regressions run using levels for 1960 and 1970, a statistically significant relationship is evident. When changes (1960–70) in basic needs indicators are regressed on changes in per capita GNP, however, only 5 of 16 regressions exhibit a significant relationship.

14. The classic discussions of three-stage least-squares estimation can be found in Zellner and Theil (1962) and Madansky (1964).

15. The subscript $\{t - k\}$ indicates that the relevant schooling index is some weighted combination of indices which terminates k periods in the past.

16. It should be noted that although factors have been identified as capital- or labour-augmenting in the discussion of specification, they are indistinguishable from 'neutral' sources of technical change in the Cobb–Douglas specification.

17. Complete discussions of these and related issues can be found in Reutlinger and Selowsky (1975).

18. Recent examples of relevant work can be found in King (1980), Knight (1979), and Knight and Sabot (1980). Sabot has recently extended this work in a massive study of the interrelations among educational inputs, cognitive skills, and subsequent job performance in Kenya and Tanzania. Preliminary results available at the time of this writing suggest that more flexible labour market arrangements in Kenya have permitted superior utilization of labour at equivalent educational levels.

As noted above, the accumulation of this sort of evidence may eventually generate a model of interaction between institutions and labour productivity changes which is sufficiently well articulated for quantification. While a comparison of two countries can be effected without any attempt to quantify 'institutional difference' as a variable, the same thing is obviously not true for a large-scale cross-section exercise.

19.   Again please note that the use of '⟨⟩' denotes a rate of change.

20.   In the growth model as specified, all of the equations are over-identified. A series of dummy variables for major sub-regions were introduced in the second stage to aid in absorbing unexplained variance, since it was clear that local culture and natural conditions could have an important influence on the processes being observed. The sub-regions defined for this work were the Caribbean, Central America, the Andean countries, the rest of South America, North Africa, the Sahel, West Africa, Central Africa, East Africa, West Asia, South Asia, South-East Asia, East Asia.

21.   Clearly, the intersection samples used for estimation of the change equations are much smaller than the full set of countries. In limited samples, the risk of systematic bias is always present, but the country observations represented in the estimates in Figure 1 look remarkably like a random sample. See Appendix C for a complete list.

22.   See for example Barger (1969).

23.   For the reader who leans toward the agricultural interpretation of this result, the nutrition component has been excluded and the resulting two-equation output model estimated by 3SLS in a subsidiary exercise. The results are reported in Appendix A. Except for a reduction in explained variance as a result of the exclusion, they are very similar to the full output equation results.

24.   The oil-producing states have been excluded from all regressions in this study except for the open economy variant of the output response model. In this version, the inclusion of import growth on the right-hand side allowed for the introduction of oil producers without horrendous outlier effects. See section (iii).

25.   A complete discussion of this issue can be found in Reutlinger and Selowsky (1975).

26.   Some studies of educational performance in LDCs support the implication of this finding. Inkeles (1974) has found a significant performance gap between students from LDCs and industrial economies on equivalent examinations in recent years.

27.   Although the distribution of literacy growth data in the 1960s is relatively smooth, some unfortunate tendencies in national self-reporting seem to have cropped up in the 1970s. Reported literacy gains for Tanzania and Somalia are gross outliers in the distribution, and it seems probable that measurement and enthusiasm for adult literacy campaigns have become intertwined in the reporting for these two countries. They have been excluded from the response model because of a strong feeling on the part of the author that the kind of literacy growth which is meaningful for productivity cannot be divorced from the process of schooling. If the two countries are included in the sample, the output equation results are unaffected but the proportion of variance accounted for by the literacy equation drops by about 0.10.

28.   It should be borne in mind that the index for medical personnel has been entered as population/doctor, so that the expected value of the associated coefficient is negative in the case of life expectancy and positive in the case of the death-rate.

29.   This approach to the role of human resources in comparative advantage owes much to Balassa (1979).

30. For reasons explained earlier in this chapter, Somalia and Tanzania have been excluded from the sample used to estimate the investment equation. In addition, Argentina and Mauritania have been excluded. The reported investment increase for Argentina is obviously in error—it is absurdly large. The reported increase for Mauritania is also so large as to be an extreme outlier in the distribution, which is otherwise quite regular.

31. See Wheeler (1980).

32. It may be this 'waterfall' effect which was identified by Kirk (1974) with the attendant observation that the pace of fertility decline seemed to have accelerated in the previous decade.

33. Leibenstein (1974), p. 460.

34. Some of the most relevant historical studies are collected in Glass and Revelle (1972). Detailed historical evaluation of the concept of the Demographic Transition has proceeded at two levels. Work at the village level has been facilitated by the development of a good methodology of family reconstruction (see Coale (1965); Coale and Trussell (1974)). Such detailed micro-level work has been sufficiently sparse for generalizations to be dubious. A natural reaction has been a parallel attempt to generate regional data on fertility trends. See Coale (1975) for a summary of findings for several European countries. Demeny's work (1968) on early fertility decline in Austria-Hungary is an example of the kind of scholarship which has called into question the theory of the Demographic Transition.

35. A description of the World Fertility Survey can be found in Kendall (1979).

36. Examples of field research on the benefits and costs of children can be found in Nag et al. (1977) and Cain (1977). Mueller (1976) and Cassen (1978) have noted some of the important difficulties in generating and interpreting this kind of data. For analyses of the institutional setting of fertility behaviour see White (1976) on labour absorption in rural Java and Cain et al. (1979) on the implication of patriarchal authority for fertility in Bangladesh.

37. See particularly Becker (1965) and Schultz (1974).

38. Becker (1960) produced the seminal work in this field. See also Schultz (1969) and Becker and Lewis (1973). Recent econometric analyses inspired by the theory can be found in Schultz (1976), Rosenzweig (1976), McCabe and Rosenzweig (1976), and Rosenzweig and Evenson (1976). Critiques of the approach can be found in Leibenstein (1974) and McNicoll (1978).

39. Leibenstein (1957, 1973) was in many ways the founder of this tradition. Its other dominant scholar is undoubtedly Easterlin (1969, 1976, 1978).

40. The proximate determinants approach can be traced through the work of Sheps (1973), Freedman (1975), Leridan (1977), and Bongaarts (1978).

41. Relevant empirical studies can be found in Cochrane and Bean (1976) and Cain et al. (1979). Hollerbach (1974) has proposed a model of sequential decision-making under uncertainty which can be used as the theoretical framework for this kind of approach.

42. This point is developed in most econometric textbooks. A particularly comprehensible discussion can be found in Pindyck and Rubinfeld (1980).

43. Birdsall (1980), p. 43.

44. Again, a point in econometric theory is at issue here. If two right-hand variables are positively correlated and one is excluded from a regression equation the estimated impact of the included variable is biased upward. Since it is likely that family planning activity is correlated with the socio-economic 'demand side' variables, the implication is clear.

45. There are other proximate determinants of fertility (e.g. the prevalence of induced abortion; the acceptance of contraceptives) which could be considered in the same light as age at marriage if appropriate data were available. Unfortunately, this is not the case.

46. This subject will be pursued further in Chapter 5.

47. For the most comprehensive existing work on the impact of the income distribution on fertility, see Repetto (1979).

48. As previously noted, I refer to this as the Mauldin–Berelson index.

49. The data on female singulate age at marriage used for econometric work in this book have been supplied by the World Bank.

50. A scatter plot of the bivariate relationship between the death-rate and the fertility rate clearly shows increasing marginal responsiveness of the latter as the death-rate declines. A quadratic term has been added to control for this non-linearity.

51. A full list of intersection sample countries for the two-equation model is presented in Appendix C.

52. Mauldin and Berelson (1978) report having performed a multivariate analysis on changes which is similar in spirit to my own work. However, they do not show their results.

53. Econometricians have been trained to avoid excessive devotion to the cult of the t-statistic. In the final simultaneous estimate, the coefficient of the family planning variable has a t-statistic of 1.8, which 'qualifies' it by the standard null hypothesis at about 90 per cent confidence. The important points here, surely are: (1) theory suggests an important role for this variable and (2) the maximum likelihood estimate for its coefficient value is much larger than zero.

54. Anyone who thinks that these models truly produce 'answers' to the world's problems has only to examine them closely. Unfortunately, their equation systems are lengthy if not particularly complex, and few have taken the trouble. Such exercises are frequently ballyhooed as yielding 'counter-intuitive' results, but this always turns out to be far from the case if only the time is taken to consider the equation systems closely. A detailed criticism of such approaches can be found in Nordhaus (1973), and Cole *et al.* (1973).

55. In passing, I cannot resist pointing to a very paradoxical result. The theoretical models of both Nelson and Enke assume that the death rate is sensitive to changes in per capita income and that the birth-rate is exogenous. My results paint a very different picture: the death-rate falls for exogenous reasons, and the birth-rate falls logistically as income increases. Obviously, a model which incorporates these features can have different dynamics from those of Nelson and Enke.

56. Discussions of the trade-off between equity and efficiency in this context have encountered difficulty in drawing a precise line between 'consumption' and 'investment'. If the social objective function is expanded to include literacy, health, and nutrition, of course, the very notion of 'investment' probably has to be overhauled. Some earlier studies have attempted to examine the question of trade-offs at the aggregate level in a dynamic context. Among economists, notable efforts are due to Ahluwalia and Chenery (1974) and Adelman and Morris (1973). In work which preceded that presented here (Wheeler, 1980), I attempted a simpler set of simultaneous estimates for the 1960s with some attendant benefit-cost analysis.

57. Some would argue, in fact, that the result of a drastically lowered fertility rate would be perverse: slower output growth along with slower population growth. The most comprehensive argument of this kind can be found in Simon (1977). I will return to it in Part IV.

58. And as an economist, I can only envy the demographers for having had such a long recovery period. We had our own come-uppance much more recently.

59. Occasionally, book titles become so closely associated with ideas that they enjoy at least a brief reign as recognizable phrases. I am referring here (respectively) to the titles of well-known offerings by Meadows *et al.* (1972) and Ehrlich (1968).

60. The economic arguments in favour of moderate population expansion as an aid to growth are fully elaborated and defended in Simon (1977).

61. One of these, the work of Hazledine and Moreland, has already been discussed in Chapter 1.

62. At this point, the reader may well be wondering how seriously I expect 75-year projections of numbers like the investment rate to be taken. The projection system has been designed so that the future horizon is limited only by the modeller's sense of the absurd. The quixotic history of the projection business supports the view that the plausible horizon is not very far away, and that long range speculations should probably be shelved in the science fiction section of libraries. I agree with this view, and I offer such long range predictions here for one main reason: the sort of modelling approach which I have proposed in this book may have important implications for long-run population growth, which depends crucially on short-term fertility rates. Unquestionably, then, the 75-year projections for population should be regarded as inherently more interesting than the PQLI projections. The latter are more likely to have meaning only for a few decades into the future, since sudden changes in investment behaviour or educational policies will have large effects on predicted outcomes after no more than two decades have gone by. The predictions offered reflect certain rather arbitrary assumptions concerning the future evolution of physical and human resource investment policies in the two countries.

63. See the discussion of Open Economy econometric results in Chapter 3. These results suggest that international trade has a significant effect on domestic productivity growth in LDCs.

64. See United Nations (1975) and (1977).

65. Strictly speaking, of course, each of my population projections is a stochastic result which is surrounded by a large forecast error. In this chapter, I see no harm in taking some liberties.

BIBLIOGRAPHY

ADELMAN, I. and C. T. MORRIS, 1973, *Economic Growth and Social Equity In Developing Countries* (Stanford University Press, Stanford).

AHLUWALIA, M. and H. CHENERY, 1974, *Redistribution with Growth* (Oxford University Press, London).

BALASSA, B., 1979, 'The Changing Patterns of Comparative Advantage in Manufactured Goods', *Review of Economics and Statistics*, 61, 259–65.

BARGER, H., 1969, 'Growth in Developing Countries', *Review of Economics and Statistics*, 51, 143–8.

BARLOW, R. and G. DAVIES, 1974, 'Policy Analysis with a Disaggregated Economic-Demographic Model', *Journal of Public Economics*, 3, 43–70.

BASTA, S. and A. CHURCHILL, 1974, *Iron Deficiency Anemia and the Productivity of Adult Males in Indonesia* (IBRD, Washington, DC).

BECKER, G., 1960, 'An Economic Analysis of Fertility', in *National Bureau of Economic Research, Demographic and Economic Changes in Developed Countries* (Princeton University Press, Princeton).

—— 1965, 'A Theory of the Allocation of Time', *Economic Journal*, 75, 493–517.

—— and H. LEWIS, 1973, 'On the Interaction Between Quantity and Quality of Children', *Journal of Political Economy*, 81, S279–88.

BERELSON, B., W. MAULDIN, and S. SEGAL, 1979, 'Background Paper on Population', for the Conference on Health and Population in Developing Countries, April 18–21, Bellagio, Italy.

BIRDSALL, N., 1980, *Population and Poverty in the Developing World* (IBRD, WDR Background Paper).

BLANDY, R. and R. WERY, 1973, 'Population and Employment Growth: Bachue-1', *International Labor Review*, 107, 441–9.

BLAUG, M., 1973, *Education and the Employment Problem in Less Developed Countries* (ILO, Geneva).

BONGAARTS, J., 1978, 'A Framework for Analyzing the Proximate Determinants of Fertility', *Population and Development Review*, 4, 105–32.

BURKI, S. J. and J. J. C. VOORHOEVE, 1977, 'Global Estimates for Meeting Basic Needs: Background Paper' (IBRD, Policy Planning and Review Department, Washington, DC).

CAIN, M., 1977, 'The Economic Activities of Children in a Village in Bangladesh', *Population and Development Review*, 3, 201–28.

——, S. KHANAM, and S. NAHAR, 1979, 'Class, Patriarchy, and the Structure of Women's Work in Rural Bangladesh', *Population and Development Review*, 5, 405–38.

CASSEN, R., 1978, *India: Population, Economy, and Society* (Holmes and Meier, New York).

COALE, A., 1965, 'Factors Associated with the Development of Low Fertility: An Historic Summary', in *Proceedings of the United Nations World Population Conference*, Belgrade (UN, New York).

— 1975, 'The Demographic Transition', in *The Population Debate: Dimensions and Perspectives* (UN, New York).

— and E. M. HOOVER, 1958, *Population Growth and Economic Development in Low Income Countries* (Princeton Press, Princeton).

— and T. TRUSSELL, 1974, 'Model Fertility Schedules: Variations in the Age Structure of Childbearing in Human Populations', *Population Index*, 40, 185–258.

COCHRANE, S., 1979, *Fertility and Education: What do we Really Know?* (Johns Hopkins University Press, Baltimore).

— and F. BEAN, 1976, 'Husband-Wife Differences in the Demand for Children', *Journal of Marriage and the Family*, 38, 297–307.

COLE, H., C. FREEMAN, M. JAHODA, K. PAVITT (eds.) 1973, *Thinking About the Future: A Critique of the Limits to Growth* (Chatto and Windus, London).

CORREA, H., 1970, 'Sources of Growth in Latin America', *Southern Economic Journal*, 37, 17–31.

DEMENY, P., 1968, 'Early Fertility Decline in Austria-Hungary: A Lesson in Demographic Transition', *Proceedings of the American Academy of Arts and Sciences*, 97, 502–22.

DENSION, E. F., 1967, *Why Growth Rates Differ* (Brookings, Washington, DC).

DYSON, T., C. G. BELL and R. H. CASSEN, 1978, 'Fertility, Mortality, and Income—Changes Over the Long Run: Some Simulation Experiments', *The Journal of Development Studies*, 4, 40–78.

EASTERLIN, R., 1969, 'Towards a Socioeconomic Theory of Fertility: A Survey of Recent Research on Economic Factors in American Fertility', in S. Behrman, L. Corsa, and R. Freedman (eds.) Fertility and Family Planning: A World View (Michigan University Press, Ann Arbor).

— 1978, 'The Economics and Sociology of Fertility: A Synthesis', in C. Tilly (ed.), *Historical Studies of Changing Fertility* (Princeton University Press, Princeton).

—, R. POLLACK, and M. WACHTER, 1976, 'Toward a More General Economic Model of Fertility Determination: Endogenous Preferences and Natural Fertility', for the NBER Conference on Economic and Demographic Change in Less Developed Countries, Sept. 30–Oct. 2, Philadelphia.

EHRLICH, P., 1968, *The Population Bomb* (Ballantine, New York).

ENKE, S., 1963, 'Population and Development: A General Model', *Quarterly Journal of Economics*, 77, 55–70.

FALLON, P. and P. LAYARD, 1975, 'Capital–Skill Complementarity, Income Distribution, and Output Accounting', *Journal of Political Economy*, April, 279–302.

FETTER, F., 1912, 'Population or Prosperity', *American Economic Review*, 3, 5-19.
FIELDS, G. S., 1980, *Education and Income Distribution in Less Developed Countries: A Review of the Literature*, (IBRD, WDR Background Paper).
FREEDMAN, R., 1975, *The Sociology of Human Fertility: An Annotated Bibliography* (Irvington, New York).
FULLER, W., 1975, 'More Evidence on Pre-Employment Vocational Training: A Case Study of a Factory in South India', World Bank Working Paper, Washington, DC.
GLASS, D. and R. REVELLE (eds.) 1972, *Population and Social Change* (Edward Arnold, London).
HANSEN, A., 1939, 'Economic Progress and Declining Population Growth', *American Economic Review*, 29, 1-15.
HAYAMI, Y. and V. RUTTAN, 1970, 'Agricultural Productivity Differences Among Countries', *American Economic Review*, 60, 895-911.
HAZLEDINE, T. and R. MORELAND, 1977, 'Population and Economic Growth: A World Cross-Section Study', *Review of Economics and Statistics*, 59, 253-63.
HICKS, N., 1979, 'A Note on the Linkages Between Basic Needs and Growth' (IBRD, Policy Planning and Program Review Department, Washington, DC).
HOLLERBACH, P., 1974, 'Wanted and Unwanted Pregnancies: A Fertility Decision-Making Model', *Journal of Social Issues*, 30, 125-65.
INKELES, A., 1974, 'The International Evaluation of Educational Achievement', *Proceedings of the National Academy of Education*, 4, 139-200.
INTRILIGATOR, M. D., 1965, 'Embodied Technical Change and Productivity in the United States, 1929-58', *Review of Economics and Statistics*, 47, 65-70.
KENDALL, M., 1979, 'The World Fertility Survey: Current Status and Findings', *Population Reports*, 3-M.
KEYNES, J. 1923, 'A Reply to Sir William Beveridge', *Economic Journal*, 33, 447-75.
— 1937, 'Some Economic Consequences of a Declining Population', *Eugenics Review*, 29, 13-17.
KING, T. (ed.) 1980, 'Education and Income', World Bank Staff Working Paper No. 407, Washington, DC.
KIRK, D., 1974. 'A New Demographic Transition?' in *National Academy of Sciences, Rapid Population Growth: Consequences and Policy Implications* (Johns Hopkins University Press, Baltimore).
KNIGHT, J., 1979, 'Job Competition, Occupational Production Functions, and Filtering Down', *Oxford Economic Papers*, 31.
— and R. SABOT, 1980, 'Why Wages Differ: A Study of Tanzania's Manufacturing Sector', World Bank Working Paper.

KOH, T., 1977, 'Education, Entrepreneurial Formation, and Entre-
preneurial Behaviour in Japan', Ph.D. Dissertation, University of
Chicago.
KUZNETS, S., 1973, *Population, Capital, and Growth* (Norton, New
York).
LEIBENSTEIN, H. 1957, *Economic Backwardness and Economic
Growth* (Wiley, New York).
— 1973, 'The Economic Theory of Fertility Decline', *Harvard Center
for Population Studies, Research Papers Series.*
— 1974, 'An Interpretation of the Economic Theory of Fertility:
Promising Path or Blind Alley?' *Journal of Economic Literature*,
12, 457-79.
LERIDON, H. 1977, *Human Fertility: The Basic Components* (Uni-
versity of Chicago Press, Chicago).
MADANSKY, A., 1964, 'On the Efficiency of Three-Stage Least
Squares Estimation', *Econometrica*, 32, 55.
MALTHUS, T., 1798/1959, *Population: The First Essay* (Michigan
University Press, Ann Arbor).
MAULDIN, W. and B. BERELSON, 1978, 'Conditions of Fertility
Decline in Developing Countries, 1965-75', *Studies in Family
Planning*, 9, 90-147.
MCCABE, J. and M. ROSENZWEIG, 1976, 'Female Labor Force
Participation, Occupational Choice, and Fertility in Developing
Countries', *Journal of Development Economics*, 3, 141-60.
MCNICOLL, G., 1978, 'Population and Development: Outlines for a
Structuralist Approach', *Journal of Development Studies*, 14,
79-99.
MEADOWS, D., D. MEADOWS, J. RANDERS, and W. BEHRENS
III, 1972, *The Limits to Growth* (Potomac Associates, New York).
MORAWETZ, D., 1977, *Twenty-Five Years of Economic Develop-
ment* (Johns Hopkins University Press, Baltimore).
— 1978, 'Basic Needs Policies and Population Growth', *World De-
velopment*, 6, 1251-9.
MUELLER, E., 1976, 'The Economic Value of Children in Peasant
Agriculture', in R. Ridker (ed.) *Population and Development: The
Search for Selective Interventions* (Johns Hopkins University Press,
Baltimore).
NAG, M., R. PEET, and B. WHITE, 1977, 'The Economic Value of
Children in Two Peasant Societies', in *International Population
Conference, Mexico 1977*, Vol. 1 (IUSSP, Liège).
NELSON, R., 1956, 'A Theory of the Low-Level Equilibrium Trap in
Underdeveloped Economies', *American Economic Review*, 46,
894-908.
NORDHAUS, W., 1973, 'World Dynamics: Measurement Without
Data', *Economic Journal*, 83, 1156-83.
PERLMAN, M., 1975, 'Some Economic Growth Problems and the Part
Population Policy Plays', *Quarterly Journal of Economics*, 89, 247-56.

PHELPS, E., 1972, 'The Macroeconomics of Population Leveling', in *U.S. Commission on Population Growth and the American Future, Final Report: Population and the American Future* (U.S. Government Printing Office, Washington, DC).

PINDYCK, R. and RUBINFELD, D. 1981, *Econometric Models and Economic Forecasts* (McGraw-Hill, New York).

PSACHAROPOULOS, G., 1973, *Returns to Education* (Jossey-Bass, San Francisco).

ROBINSON, S., 1971, 'Sources of Growth in Less Developed Countries: A Cross-Section Study', *Quarterly Journal of Economics*, 85, 391–408.

ROSENZWEIG, M., 1976, 'Female Work Experience, Employment Status, and Birth Expectations: Sequential Decision-Making in the Philippines', *Demography*, 13, 339–56.

— and R. EVENSON, 1977, 'Fertility, Schooling, and the Economic Contribution of Children in Rural India: An Econometric Analysis', *Econometrica*, 45, 1065–80.

SAXONHOUSE, G. R., 1977, 'Productivity Change and Labor Absorption in Japanese Cotton Spinning, 1891–1935', *Quarterly Journal of Economics*, 91, 195–219.

SCHULTZ, T. P., 1969, 'An Economic Model of Family Planning and Fertility', *Journal of Political Economy*, 77, 153–80.

— 1976, 'Interrelationships Between Mortality and Fertility', in R. Ridker (ed.), *Population and Development: The Search for Selective Interventions* (Johns Hopkins University Press, Baltimore).

SCHULTZ, T. W. (ed.) 1974, *Economics of the Family: Marriage, Children, and Human Capital* (University of Chicago Press, Chicago).

SCRIMSHAW, S., 1978, 'Infant Mortality and Behavior in the Regulation of Family Size', *Population and Development Review*, 4, 383–403.

SELOWSKY, M., 1969, 'On the Measurement of Education's Contribution to Growth', *Quarterly Journal of Economics*, 83, 449–63.

SHEPS, M. and J. MENKEN, 1973, *Mathematical Models of Conception and Birth*, (University of Chicago Press, Chicago).

SIMON, J., 1974, 'The Effects of Income on Fertility', Carolina Population Center Monograph No. 19 (University of North Carolina, Chapel Hill).

— 1977, *The Economics of Population Growth*, (Princeton University Press, Princeton).

UNITED NATIONS, 1975, 'Selected World Demographic Indicators by Countries, 1950–2000', Report ESA/P/WP/55 (UN, New York).

— 1977, 'World Population Prospects as Assessed in 1973', Report ST/ESA/SER.A/60 (UN, New York).

VON THUNEN, J., 1966, *The Isolated State* (Pergamon, New York).

WHEELER, D., 1980, 'Basic Needs Fulfillment and Economic Growth: A Simultaneous Model', *Journal of Development Economics*, 7, 435–51.

WHEELER, D., 1980, 'Human Resource Development and Economic Growth in LDCs (IBRD, WDR Background Report).

WHITE, B., 1976, 'Population, Involution, and Employment in Rural Java', *Development and Change*, 7, 267–90.

WORLD BANK, 1980, *World Development Report* (IBRD, Washington DC).

ZELLNER, A., and H. THEIL, 1962, 'Three-Stage Least Squares: Simultaneous Estimation of Simultaneous Relations', *Econometrica*, 30, 54–78.

INDEX